ANCIENT GREECE

Text by G. BEJOR, University of Pisa - Italy
Reconstruction: Vision S.r.l.
Layout: U. Ulivieri - F. Schneider

1st edition 1997
New edition 2010

ISBN 978-88-8162-271-9

Distributed in Greece by

MICHALIS TOUBIS S.A.
EDITIONS - GRAPHIC ARTS

P.C.: 194 00 P.O. Box 209. Tel: +30210 6029974, +30210 6645548
Fax: +30210 6646856, e-mail: info@toubis.gr, http://www.toubis.gr

Printed in Italy by: Tipolitografica CS - Padova

INTRODUCTION

The historians of ancient times named the first inhabitants of Greece Pelasgous. The archaeological findings in Sesklo and Dimini in Thessaly have brought to knowledge a population that already since the IV millennium BC had reached a significant level of civilization, cultivated the land and produced pottery. Between 2500 and 2000 BC, Pelasgoi were joined by the Achaeans, races from the Balkans that expanded in continental Greece. Almost at the same time, other races from the East settled in Crete, which later met great growth. In the early 2nd millennium these races formed local societies under the rule of kings who lived in the imposing palaces of Knossos, Faestos and Mallia. Around 1700 these palaces were destroyed, probably due to earthquakes; however, the island's extensive economic activities made possible their immediate reconstruction. Thus began the most glorious phase of this civilization which was termed Minoan after the name of the mythical king Minos. The palaces are now decorated with magnificent frescoes and, thanks to trade, the Cretan ships dominate the Aegean and the neighboring countries.

Between 1450 and 1400 BC this civilization comes abruptly to an end. After subsequent earthquakes and especially the explosion of the Santorini volcano, the Minoan civilization is utterly destroyed and Achaean races invade Crete. Certain cities in the islands and the continent maintain their progress; these cities had grown under the Minoan sphere of influence and they now give their place to the civilization which was termed Mycenaean, after its most important centre, the city of Mycenae. Walled acropolises and glorious tombs signify its great wealth. But even here, around 1200 BC, several signs of arson and damages indicate the arrival of the first waves of new invaders. In the next century, everything is overturned; it seems that in this way the first invasion of the Greek terrain by the Dories took place, an invasion known and mentioned by the ancient historians.

Since then, in the whole of Greece, a dark period begins: the inhabitants become fewer and abandon the cities, people live off farming in villages and poor huts, pottery gradually becomes plain. These are the dark years of the alleged Greek Middle Ages.

In the beginning of 1000 BC one can observe signs of improvement in several places.

There is again a population growth and trade is resumed, thus bringing about the rebirth of the cities.

Trade is originally confined to the Aegean and the Eastern coasts up to North Syria; later, by following the ancient marine routes drawn by the Mycenaeans, the trading ships visit the West. In the 8th century BC, merchants from Euboea reach the Tyrrenean Sea where they found Iskia, the ancient Pithykousa. This city is the first in a series of new cities which were founded and established in Greek territory but which were unable to cope with the great demographic explosion.

During the same period certain Sanctuaries, such as these of Delphi, Olympia and Delos, gain increasing importance. With these sanctuaries as a focal point, alliances of cities are created. Sparta, Athens, Corinth, Megara, Argos, Thebes and many more cities have now become big and wealthy trade centres with significantly differentiated populations within which there emerge the first social tensions. Thus, it becomes necessary to formulate the first legal regulations, such as those of Dracon and Solon in democratic Athens and that of Lycourgos in oligarchic Sparta. Other cities, such as Corinth, Megara and Argos shift from primitive monarchies to aristocracies and later, in some cases, even to tyrannies. In the case of Athens, in 561 BC Pisistratos seized power and democracy was not restored until 510 BC.

Around the end of the 9th century BC, the great cities in the eastern coasts of the Aegean are forced to start considering the expansion of a new considerable Asian power, that of the Persian kingdom. In 549 BC Kyro annexed Lydia to Persia and subjugated many Greek colonies. A big uprising, headed by the city of Militos, ended with the destruction of the city in 494 BC. In order to punish Greece for helping the revolutionaries, the new king Darius embarked on a big military expedition against Greece. Through the Ellyspontos he reached Thrace, Macedonia and Thessaly and collided with the joined Greek forces in Marathon in 490 BC. During this astounding battle, the Persians were utterly defeated and withdrew. Ten years later Darius' son, Xerxes, resumed military expeditions against Greece. In 480 BC the outnumbering Persian forces collided with 300 Spartans guided by Leonidas in Thermopilae. The monument at this spot reminds visitors today of that unfortunate battle and of the famous sacrifice of the 300 soldiers. Xerxes continued his descent to Athens while destroying and pillaging. The population suffered a lot and the Holy City itself was pillaged to a large extent. And while the Persian army was destroying the attic land, the Persian navy attempted to cut-off Athens at the beginning of 480 BC; however, the Persian navy was defeated by the Greek one during the historical and glorious sea-battle of Salamis. The next year, 479 BC, Athenians and Spartans joined forces and finally destroyed the Persian land forces in Plataeae.

Athens gained the most from these great victories. Under the rule of Pericles, she managed to attract in alliance – which originally had as its centre the Apollo Sanctuary in Delos – many Aegean islands (462-449 BC) and later she attempted to reconstruct the monuments of Acropolis which had been destroyed and pillaged by the Persians. Thus began the famous Golden Age of Pericles. In every respect, this was a time of great growth and prestige concerning Man, arts, literature and philosophy and civilization in general.

In 445 BC, the two great powers, Athens and Sparta, had signed a peace treaty. However, between 433 and 431 BC, certain disputes concerning Corfu, Potoidaea and Megara led to a long war that spread to the whole of Greece and even to the coasts of Minor Asia and Sicily. This war lasted for thirty years and it is known as the Peloponnesian War.

At the end of the war in 404 BC, the surrender of Athens left the city deserted. Victorious Sparta imposed on the defeated cities oligarchic governments, an act that caused further uprisings. Athens, together with Argos, Thebes and Corinth by slowly but progressively returning to more democratic forms of government, managed to considerably reduce Spartan control. The war between the coalition of these cities against Sparta – known as the Corinthian war – ended in 386 BC.

While Athens once more heads a new marine alliance, Thebes overturns the government cooperating with the Spartans and restores democracy with the coalition of Boeotian cities. A Spartan military corps which was sent against them was vanquished in Leuktra in 371 BC by the Thebeans headed by Epaminondas and Pelopidas. Arcadians and Messenians seized the opportunity to reclaim their independence from Sparta by asking the support of Thebes. This was the beginning of the brief Theban hegemony in Greece. Already in 362 BC, however, during another expedition in Peloponnese, Epaminondas was killed in the battle of Mantinea. In addition, there were wars within each alliance such as the alleged "social war of the Athenians" (357-354 BC) or the "holy war" between the Fokaeans, the Thessaleans and the Boeotians for the control of the Delphi (356-346 BC).

This last war marked the emergence in the course of history of a new power, that of the kingdom of Macedonia which, until then, had played only a secondary part in the Peloponnesian War. After a period of disputes between tyrants, in 359 BC, the throne passed to Philip II. He first defeated the Illyrians and later the Athenians at the Chalkidiki peninsula; he then took part in the "holy war" supporting the Thessaleans. The victories led to the Filokratean peace, which marks the beginning of the Macedonian sovereignty. This sovereignty became indisputable after the defeat the allied forces of the Atheneans and the Thebeans suffered in Chaeronia in 338 BC by Philip's forces. Philip is getting prepared for the great expedition against Persia when in 336 BC he falls victim of a conspiracy within the palace.

He is succeeded by his son Alexander who was only twenty years old.

Alexander very quickly subjugated the Illyrians who had revolted and suppressed the insurrection of the Greek cities, by utterly destroying the city of Thebes apart from the Sanctuaries and the house of the great poet Pindarus. In 334 BC he headed the big expedition against the Persians, previously planned by his father. Within a few years he repeatedly crushed the Asian forces, reached the Indus river and installed Greek governors at the conquered cities, which spanned to a vast territory. However, in 323 BC he found a sudden death in Babylon at the young age of 33.

At the wars fought by his generals in order to distribute between them his vast kingdom, despite the attempts made by the strongest cities to regain their independence, the role of Greece has been marginal: even the city of Athens was forced to accept a Macedonian patrol. During the next years, in order to resist the conquering plans of Macedonia, certain confederations were formed and gained power, namely the Achaean and the Aetolian confederation. Aside these confederations and certain other cities that were fighting to check the Macedonian wave came Rome, which had already since 229 BC deprived the Illyrians of the control over Corfu. In 197 BC Titus Cointus Flaminius defeated Philip V of Macedonia at the Kynos Kephales in Tessaly and the next year he declared the independence of all the Greek cities. This independence, however, was illusory, since the cities were under Roman "protection". A second battle against the Macedonians at Pydna in 168 BC proved to be a great triumph for the Romans. Macedonia, together with a part of Epirus and Illyria, became a Roman province. The same happened to Central Greece after a subsequent war that lasted from 149 to 146 BC and ended with the destruction of Corinth. Once more, Athens and the other cities kept their independence nominally; however, the Roman rule was so despised that in 88 BC all these cities participated in the uprising of Mithridates, king of Pontos. Once more, the defeat was devastating: in 86 BC, Sylla ruined Athens and slaughtered her inhabitants. Since then, Greece finally and decisively came under Roman occupation. The country was forced to simply recall the memories of her great cultural and artistic traditions and was unable to play any significant part. The special attention shown to her by certain emperors, such as Nero and Hadrian as well as personalities such as Herodes Atticus added new monuments to her collection and gave her a new period of apparent peak. From the beginning of the II century AD however, subsequent barbarian invasions worsened things: in 170 AD the Kostobokians destroyed Eleusis and in 267 AD the Goths and the Erouls pillaged the Holy City of Athens and the Peloponnese and annihilated their inhabitants.

After the establishment of Constantinople in 323 AD, the country became in effect a periphery of the new capital, thus quickly losing even its cultural precedence. The ancient monuments were abandoned, whereas many of the most glorious statues were transported to the new capital.

PLAN OF THE ACROPOLIS INCLUDING THE MOST IMPORTANT MONUMENTS

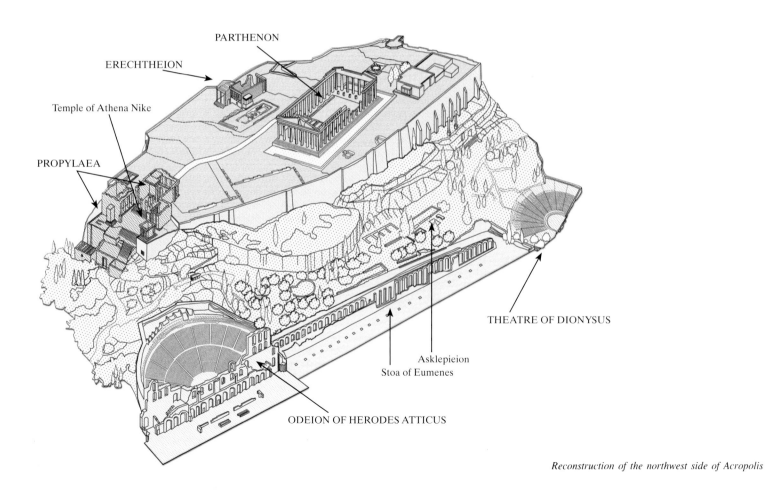

PARTHENON

ERECHTHEION

Temple of Athena Nike

PROPYLAEA

THEATRE OF DIONYSUS

Asklepieion
Stoa of Eumenes

ODEION OF HERODES ATTICUS

Reconstruction of the northwest side of Acropolis

ATHENS

Contemporary Athens takes up almost the whole flat area **ATHENS** between the Saronicos Gulf and the mountains of Athens. At the centre of this mythical area appears the imposing site where the sacred heartbeat of the city continues to sound after many centuries: the limestone rock of Acropolis. Around this rock were born and took place the most ancient myths and it is here where the legendary king Theseus lived. Fortified with high walls from the mycenean times, around 550 BC at the time of Pisistratos a palatial residence was built there and served as a place for the worship of gods, whose ruins are still visible today. Since then numerous temples and statues were continuously being added. After 480 BC, when the Persians literally ruined the sacred rock of Acropolis, within a small span of time, all the buildings were reconstructed and this reconstruction became the symbol of the triumph of Athens. Pericles, the leader of the city at that period, gathered the biggest artists of his time under the guidance of a genius "supervisor", Phidias. Within a few years Acropolis took this grandiose form that established her as a unique jewel and a symbol of the attic moderation in the world, as well as one of the most glorious masterpieces in the western world. To the existing monuments were added a new splendid temple of the Virgin Athena, the Parthenon, as well as the great imposing entrance, the Propylaea. Later, the small temple of Athena Nike was added, whereas near the north edge of the rock, some of the oldest deities were hosted in a peculiar building, the Erechtheion. During the later roman period, and even more so during the Middle Ages, the Acropolis was once again used for what was initially built, that is, as a fortress: new defensive measures surrounded the classical buildings, in one way hiding them but in another way protecting them. However, the sacred marbles suffered many damages caused by the collisions between the Turkish conquerors and the Venetians. During repeated invasions many of them were stolen, such as a considerable part of the statues and the friezes allegedly called the Elgin Marbles, after the name of the British Lord who in the early 19th century removed them and shipped them to London where they still are. After the emancipation of Greece from the Turkish rule, in 1832, a purification of the ancient buildings from added edifices took place and after subsequent archaeological excavations and restorations the Acropolis took its current face. Recently, a new danger, that of pollution of the urban atmosphere, made necessary the replacement of certain original sculptures with duplicates.

THE ACROPOLIS. The only way of getting to the top of the sacred rock had always been from the west side: in every other side, the steep slopes had served as an inaccessible natural fort, although as early as in the mycenean period they had been externally reinforced and later, in the 5th century BC, both Themistocles and Cimon used for the same purpose the large concrete pieces of poros stone that emerged from the damages caused by the Persians. Today, one can climb the sacred rock via a very old uphill slope through the ruins of the large external scale added by the Romans. The massive and crude arch Beulé (after the French archaeologist who discovered it in 1852) is an earlier addition. This arch was built by the Romans

The Propylaea on 5th century BC

The Temple of Athena Nike, work of Kallikrates

during the third century AD, at the time of the German invasions, in order to avert any possibility of approaching the Acropolis.

Later, at the left edge of the same side, there was added the great monument made of Hymettus marble that looks like a tower: on the top, there was probably the chariot with four horses of king Pergamos, which was later replaced by the statues of Anthony and Cleopatra and later again by the statue of Agrippa, son-in-law of Augustus, who ordered the inscription one can read today.

At the top of the uphill, already since the mycenean times, the entrance was protected by battlements which were later replaced by a glorious passage, the Propylon. During the construction of the sacred rock undertaken by Phidias, this passage gave its place to a rectangle edifice which was conceived as highlighting the holiness of the space. Through its main hall, which also served as its main entrance, passed the Sacred Way, the path followed by the great procession of Panathinaea: this entrance are the **Propylaea**. Their construction began in 435 BC under the supervision of the architect Mnesicles. Three years later, the works which, according to the

Nike untying her sandal.
From the architrave of the temple of Athena Nike

The Parthenon: reconstruction

inscriptions found in excavations had cost 2000 talanta, were abruptly suspended at the beginning of the Peloponnesian War and they were never actually completed. The marble used was mainly from Penteli combined, especially around the entrance, with the grey eleusiniac marble in such a way that there is an interruption in the monotony of white colour and an emphasis on certain characteristic architectural elements.

On each side of the main rectangle building there are two wings, one at the North and one at the South, which are uneven in dimensions, according to the tradition of sacred spaces.

The main building measures 18.20x25 metres and has six Doric pillars 8.81 metres high at the façade; these pillars support an architrave frieze and pediment like in all temples. Two rows of

North side of the frieze: detail from a sacrificial procession

The Hydriaphorae

The interior of the Parthenon with the statue of Athena Parthenos of Phidias: reconstruction

Ionic pillars run through the interior space, interrupted by the scale that leads to the Acropolis. A wall divides the temple into two façades, an eastern and a western, which, in order for the temple to conform with the inclination of the slopes, are covered with roofs of unequal height. The magnificent marble sculptures that adorned the roofs had been deeply admired by the ancient world. On each side of the entrance's prostylon, each of the two wings was designed in such a way as to give the impression of a building with three doric pillars; however, only the northern wing was completed. At this wing there were paintings of the great artists of the era, such as Polygnotos, and for that reason it was called *Pinakotheke*. As mentioned before, the south side remained simply a small prostylon with three pillars, beyond which there was no other housed space, but only the passage to the balcony upon which the **Temple of Athena Nike** was built.

This is a small temple with porticos at both ends, measuring 8.27x5.44 metres, with four Ionic pillars of 4.66 metres high on both its front as well as its back. Its construction lasted several years and was completed after 430 BC by Kallikrates. It was built on the ruins of a mycenaean tower which was at the time covered with limestone blocks.

In its interior there was the ancient "xoanon", that is the wooden statue of Apteros Nike. On the architraves, a linear frieze of twenty five metres total length adorned all four sides. A part of the frieze is now at the British Museum and in their place there are duplicates. On the east side, the frieze portrayed the gods of Olympus standing with Athena between Zeus and Poseidon. On the other sides battles between Greeks and Amazons or between Greeks and Persians are portrayed.

Even the pediments must have been adorned, probably with representations of the Amazonomachia or

Detail of the procession from the western frieze

Athena Parthenos, from the Varvakeion
(Athens, Nat. Arch. Museum)

Erechtheion: reconstruction of the northeastern side

the Gigantomachia (wars between the Giants). Around 410 BC around the bulwark's kerb it was built a stylobate decorated with reliefs, some of which are today in the Museum of the Acropolis. They depicted winged Nikes in various positions, others with their dresses stuck on their bodies as if wet and others with their wings open so delicately sculptured, that they gave the impression that they were flying; these reliefs indeed are ideal examples of the alleged *luxurious order*.

Coming out of the Propylaea, at the same angle and at the most conspicuous spot of the sacred rock of the Acropolis one can see the imposing temple of the goddess Athena, the Parthenon. Once, directly in front of the Propylaea there rose the colossal brass statue of Promachos Athena, i.e. the goddess prepared to fight

Erechtheion: the Caryatid Porch

in order to protect her city. This work of Phidias was 7.50 metres tall and reflected under the sun in order to be seen by the sailors who wished to reach the port of Piraeus. On the south side of the rock there were the Temeni of Hygeia (Health) and of Artemis Brauronia, as well as the Calcotheke, as it was called, where the brass offerings were kept. Opposite, at the north edge, there were some of the oldest sanctuaries: the grottos of Apollo and Pan, the sanctuary of the nymph Aglauros with its deep well which was opened in the mycenaean period, as well as the house of the Arreforae, the virgin girls who had to weave Athena's veil. During the Panathinaea ceremonies the virgins had to bring the veil to the goddess. They set off from Kerameikos, at the northwestern side of the city, crossed the Agora, came up through the Propylaea and followed the winding route of the Sacred Way through the Erechtheion and the edge of the Parthenon's northern side, in order to end up in front of the south side.

At this spot rose high walls marking a large terrain comprising the ruins of the monuments the Persians had destroyed in 480 BC. During

Archaic pediment with the three-bodied monster (Acropolis Museum)

the excavations undergone in the previous century, this spot proved to be a rare source of ancient sculptures: most of them are offerings and decorations of temples of the period between 550 and 480 BC, which are kept today in the Acropolis Museum. Pausanias, who visited the Acropolis soon after 150 AD mentions in his invaluable writings that he saw the whole plateau covered with offering statues.

Today, in the plain and rocky landscape stands out the gigantic and imposing volume of the **Parthenon**. This is the holiest of all the monuments in Athens, already famous in antiquity as a masterpiece of the Greek architecture and the attic moderation. Its construction began in 447 BC upon the ruins of an earlier temple of the goddess, which was destroyed by the Persians. The architect of the Parthenon was Iktinos, but Phidias himself supervised the works and undertook the sculptures decorating the temple. The inauguration took place in 438 BC, whereas it was completed in 432. It was kept almost unchanged up until the sixth century AD. Later, in 1400 AD it was converted into a Christian temple, then into a mosque and finally into an ammunition storage place, still keeping the largest part of its marbles. In 1687, after being cannonaded by the Venetian doge Morosini, a large part of the temple was destroyed. In 1803 many of its marbles were removed by Lord Elgin and were transported to London. When the Greeks regained their independence, the Parthenon, as well as the rest of the Acropolis was relieved of all the medieval and Turkish additions. In 1930 the whole of the north colonnade was restored; however, the restoration works continue up to the present. Made entirely from Pentelic marble, it stands on a stylobate with three levels. It has eight Doric pillars at the small and 17 at each one of its large sides, 10.43 metres high and with a base diameter of 1.905 metres; its overall dimensions were 69.54x30.87 metres. The impression of absolute harmony is achieved thanks to the genius sequence of the relationships between its constituent parts, as well as thanks to the inspired use of almost imperceptible visual corrections. Thus, the stylobate has an approximately 7 centimetre inclination (in 70 metres!), the main body of the pillars between the base and the capital is enlarged for about the two thirds of its height and slightly sloping towards the centre of the building, the corner pillars are slightly larger and closer to their next and so on.

The Moschophoros and the small Kore from Chios (Acropolis Museum)

On the pillars there were the architraves which supported the Doric pediment decorated with alternated triglyphs and detailed metopes, whose themes were worked out by Phidias in his workshop. On the western side, the metopes depicted scenes from the Amazonomachia, on the northern side scenes from the Trojan War, on the southern side scenes from the Centauromachia and on the eastern side, above the main entrance, scenes from the Gigantomachia, the battle between the gods and the Giants. Although many of the metopes were lost, some can still be seen at their places, whereas others are in London and Paris.

The two smaller sides ended in pediments, once again decorated with Phidias' sculptures. At the western pediment, which is visible from the Propylaea, is depicted the race between Athena and Poseidon for the name of the city. Between them there was the branch of olive tree, the gift of the victorious Athena. Presently, from this pediment one can only see a few signs, but it is known enough from the plans drawn before the cannonade of Morosini took place.

The eastern pediment depicted the birth of Athena from Zeus' head with the other gods of Olympus watching the scene. Exceptional are the statues of Dionysus, lying down at the left corner, and that of Aphrodite, sitting nonchalantly at the other side, wearing a beautiful dress. Both these statues, as well as most of the others, are presently at the British Museum. At the tips of the pediments one can admire the magnificent work of Phidias: on the left appear, strong and exuberant, two heads of the horses of Helios' (Sun) chariot, whereas on the right almost disappears a horse's head from the chariot of Selini (Moon). At the temple's interior, a straight corridor separates the 46 pillars around the hall from the temple's wall. At this corridor, one could see a linear frieze (160 m), probably the most famous of Phidias' works, which surrounded the upper part of the temple. This frieze carries through history the impression of the Panathinaic procession which took place every four years during the month Hecatombaion (15 July-15 August) and lasted for twelve days. The procession begins from the northwestern corner with the gathered riders in Kerameikos and unfolds in every side with the numerous pictures of those participating in the ceremonies, and ends in the middle of the eastern side, above the main entrance of the temple, with the offering of the veil to the goddess. The largest part of these reliefs as well is today in London and only a few, such as the scenes from the preparations of the riders before the beginning of the procession, remain to their places.

The cella had six Doric pillars on each of its smaller sides, whereas its interior was divided into four parts and served as a place for keeping the most precious offerings made to the goddess. The Eastern side was its most sacred part. It was one hundred attic feet long (approximately 30 metres) and two rows divided it into three large naves; the central nave ended in three pillars which surrounded the colossal, almost 15 metres high, golden and ivory statue of Athena Parthenos, another work by Phidias. The statue's skeleton was wooden, the bare members ivory, whereas the clothes and the military equipment were covered with forged gold leaf. The goddess was standing, wearing on her bosom the miraculous aegis with the gorgon and on her

Kritios' Boy, sculpture in a severe style (c. 480 BC, Acropolis Museum)

head the attic helmet decorated with sphinxes and winged horses. With the right hand she held a Nike supporting herself on a pillar. With the left hand she held her shield which bent over the ground. A representation of the Gigantomachia decorated the inner part of the shield, together with the tutelary serpent of the Acropolis, whereas the outer side picture a battle against the Amazons. Phidias was accused for impiety, allegedly for having included himself as a balding old man and Pericles as an infantryman among the Greeks who had defeated the Amazons. Even the soles of Athena's huge sandals were decorated with a Centauromachia, whereas the relief base of the statue depicted the birth of Pandora, in gold figures applied on the marble surface. In 426 BC the statue was transported to Constantinople where, according to one version, it was destroyed in a fire. Today we can have a very precise image of how it looked like, both from numerous descriptions as well as from several archaic copies in smaller dimensions.

Between the Parthenon and the Erechtheion one can see directly on the rock the foundations of another great temple, that of Polias Athena, which was destroyed by the Persians. According to astronomers' calculations based on its orientation we can conclude that it was built in 529 BC. The decoration of the friezes which are housed in the Acropolis Museum is dated at 525 BC.

Further north, at the northern edge of Acropolis, rise the white walls of the **Erechtheion**. This is a peculiar building devoted to the worship of several old divinities. It was built of Pentelic marble during the Peloponnesian War, between 421 and 406 BC, probably by the architect Mnesicles. The temple was set on fire several times and it was respectively restored before it was converted to a Christian temple on the sixth century AD. When the Acropolis was turned into a Turkish fort, the Erechtheion was used as a lodging for the Turkish commander's harem. After Greece's independence, it was relieved of all the additions and restored to its initial form. The cella itself is a rectangle 20.03x11.21 metres with six slender Ionic pillars on the eastern side. The hall is divided into four parts; the main one, on the eastern side, contained the old statue of Athena, the *xoanon* (made of olive wood). Before the goddess burnt the famous *eternal flame*, the work of the sculptor Callimacus. The western part was also divided into three halls and contained the altars of Poseidon, of the legendary Erechtheus, of Hephaestus and that of the local hero Boutos. A small entrance led west to the yard of the temenos of the nymph Pandrossus, the Pandrosseio, where the sacred olive tree of Athens was planted. The tree that we see today at the same place was planted again in 1917. From here, a small scale led to the grave of Kekropas, the mythical king of Athens, right under the northwestern edge of the Erechtheion. On the north side, at a lower level, in conformity with the terrain which has a downward slope of about three metres there is a porch with four Ionic pillars at the façade and two at the sides. There we see a vault where probably lived the tutelary serpent, Erechtheus' sacred snake to which the Atheneans offered honey-pies every month.

The Ionic decoration of the door was grandiose; through that door, the porch communicated with the main temple. The ceiling was decorated with marble plaques, one of which had a hole which was never closed because it was said to have been made by the thunderbolt Zeus has thrown to Erechtheus. On the left side of the propylon, on the rock, there are three holes, as if they were made by Poseidon's trident, which made the rock to well up salt water.

At the opposite side, before the Parthenon, there is another porch, which instead of pillars it has six female statues of about 2.30 metres high. They were given by Vitruvius the name "Caryatids", because the sculptor had used as models girls from the city of Caryae, near Sparta. They are wearing ionic tunics and on their heads they wear a basket, which serves as the capital of the pillar. The second Kore from the left was removed by Lord Elgin and in her place there was installed a plaster cast. At present, due to the serious pollution of the atmosphere, the rest of the Caryatids are in the Acropolis Museum while they are substituted with copies.

The remarkable new museum building is located 300 meters from the south east foot of the Acropolis on Dionysiou Areopagitou; a visit here offers a panoramic experience of the ancient Greek sculpture. Here there are concentrated the limestone metopes of the temples destroyed by the Persians, many statues of young men, such as the Moschophoros (calf-bearer), the first statue in Acropolis (560 BC), busts and statues of Korae, as well as anything saved from the Persian invasion. One can also admire the preseved friezes of the Parthenon depicting the Panathinaic procession and the balustrade from the temple of Athena Nike.

Above the walls of the Acropolis the eye embraces the entire city. On the northeastern side, appear the Theatre of Dionysus on the foot of the hill and far down the pillars of the temple of Zeus Olympios and the white bulk of the Stadion which was constructed in order to host the first modern Olympic Games of 1896. On the other side rise the two Roman Agorae with Hadrian's library and the tower of the Winds and further west the Greek Agora, where lies the imposing temple of Hephaestus still in excellent condition.

THE THEATRE OF DIONYSUS. At the sixth century BC, when Pisistratos introduced in Athens the cult of Dionysus, there was built for the god a small temple on the foot of Acropolis. Around the end of the same century, at the nearby level spot the first Dionysian festivals began to take place, with musical and theatrical performances; the spectators watched these performances seated on the slope of the hill. Therefore, soon they installed wooden benches and the space where the performances were taking place was converted in such a way that it took the shape of a perfect circle. The stage adopted the name *orchestra* - from the verb *orchoumae* which means "to dance" - as the chorus danced around the *thymeli*, the god's altar. Furthermore, a wooden edifice was built in order to divide the theatre from the temple but also as a place to store the

Theatre of Dionysus: reliefs from proscaenium

The theatre of Dionysus: reconstruction

essentials for the performances. In this theatre Aeschylus, Sophocles and Euripides directed their tragedies and Aristophanes his comedies. At the fourth century BC the wooden benches were replaced by poros stone seats, some of which are preserved today. Then the theatre took its characteristic hollow shape, with 64 rows of seats which were divided by a semicircle corridor into two levels. 13 small scales extending like radiuses from the stage served as pathways to the seats. It has been calculated that the theatre could seat 17000 people. 67 benches made of Pentelic marble, many of which are saved today, constituted the first row which was reserved for the exceptional figures of the city. On the other side of the orchestra a glorious two-storey scenery structure with a row of pillars at the end of each side was erected.

During the Hellenistic period, this structure underwent many changes, one of which was the addition of a "proscaenium", which rendered the use of the big circle in the orchestra completely obsolete. During the reign of Nero, who came in 61 AD in order to participate in the music contest, the orchestra was reduced to a semicircle, whereas the façade of the proscaenium was adorned with rows of pillars later embellished with statues and reliefs. All these were destroyed during the Gothic invasions of the third century AD. A part of the sculptures, which were completed by the second century AD, were used by the Byzantine noble Phaedros in order to decorate a rostrum still preserved today: on the right side it depicts the birth of Dionysus, with Zeus seated and before him Hermes holding the divine child, as well as other scenes from the cult of Dionysus. The detailed marble floor preserved until today is also a product of the Roman period, as well as the parapet around the stage, which was considered necessary when the place started hosting duels between gladiators or even boat-races (!) after they blocked the back of the parapet and filled the orchestra with water.

THE ODEION OF HERODES ATTICUS

In 161 AD the Greek noble man Tiberius Claudius Atticus Herodes built a theatre in the memory of his wife, Aspasia Regilla. This was a roofed building that hosted music events and was thus called Odeion. The audience area, the *koilon*, consisted of 32 rows of seats and could hold around 5000 people. The audience could get to their seats through six oblong scales and five intervening ones, used for the higher seats. In the tradition of the Roman theatres, the orchestra was a semicircle and the seats communicated directly with the scenery edifice. The latter was at the back of the stage and had three storeys, two of which are still preserved. The façade was adorned with a double row of pillars, whereas the entrances were at the rear ends. Between 1950 and 1961 the audience area was restored and floored with pentelic marble whereas the orchestra with Hymettus marble, in order to be used again for performances, notably classic tragedies and comedies, a tradition still preserved every summer during the Festival of Athens.

The big portico which connects the Odeion with the Theatre of Dionysus is dated as contemporary to the

Theatre of Dionysus: reliefs from proscaenium

Odeion of Herodes Atticus: reconstruction of the stage

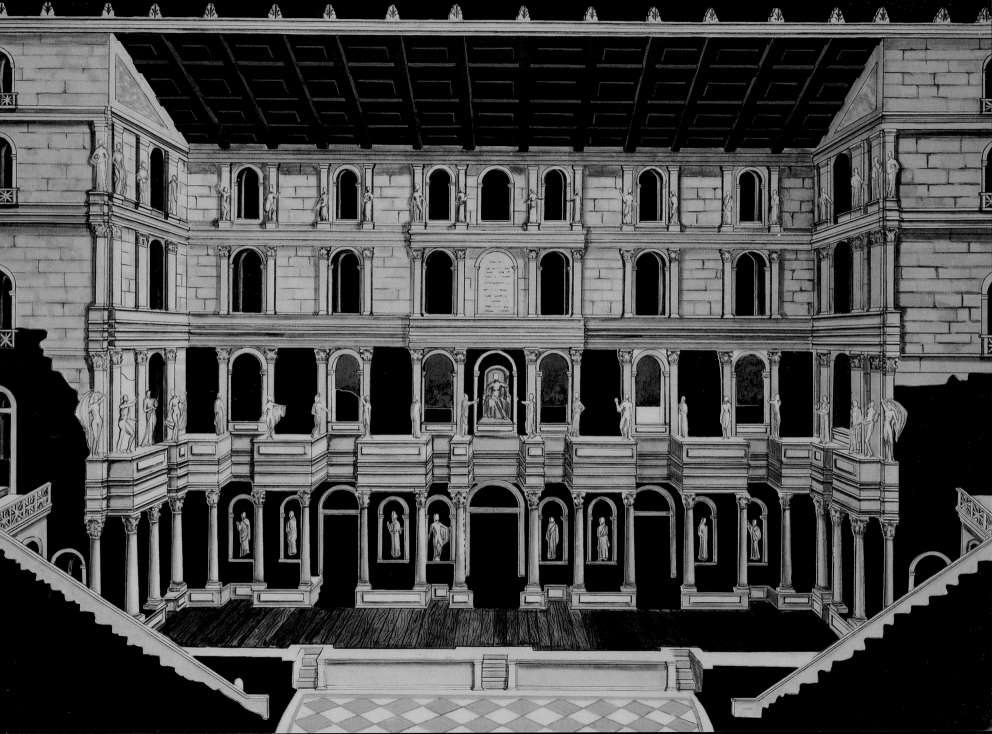

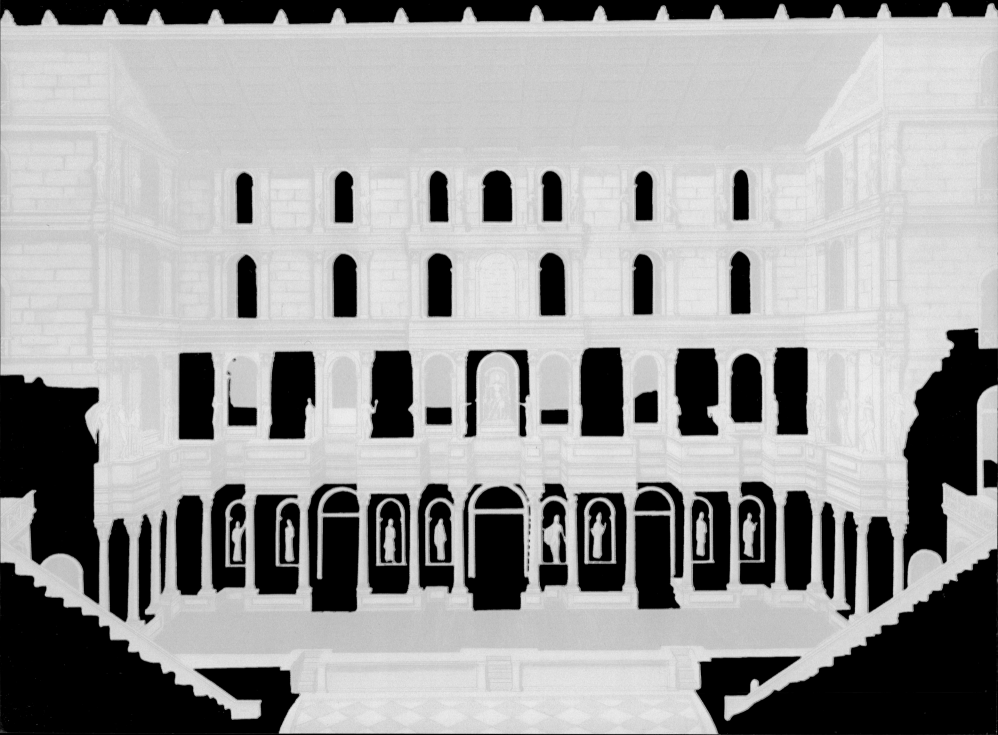

Odeion of Herodes Atticus. The portico has two naves 163 metres long and 17.65 metres wide and it is situated along the south side of the Acropolis. It has been called the Eumenes Portico after its donor, the king of Pergamos Eumenes II, a deep admirer of Athens, who lived on the second century AD. The portico served as a refuge to theatergoers in the event of bad weather. It was destroyed by the Turks when it was attached to the fort of the Acropolis, but there are still some walls preserved on the slopes of the Sacred hill.

THE AGORA. On the northwestern side of the Acropolis, between the hills of the Nymphs and the Aeropagos, during the archaic period there was a cemetery. However, from 600 BC, this space gradually became busy and not before long it was turned into the centre of Athens' public life, at the same way the Acropolis was the centre of her religious life. The Athenians gathered there and, as the word *agora* reveals, it was a meeting place for citizens, a large, open space full of buildings and people. Despite the damages it had suffered by the Persians, the Agora was restored much before Pericles' governing and it continued being adorned up to the Roman period, when the architects abandoned the concept of a central, open space and started constructing public buildings even within the site of the Agora. In 267 AD the Erouls, during one of their invasions, literally destroyed it and later, during the next 150 years, it remained a space full of ruins, outside the new walls of the city.

During the fifth century BC on the site of the Agora a large gymnasium was constructed, which was used up to the end of the next century. Then, the whole area was covered with poor establishments, similar to those still found at the neighboring Plaka.

On the West side of the archaeological site of the Agora, one can see on a hill the **Temple of**

The temple of Hephaestus

PLAN OF THE AGORA

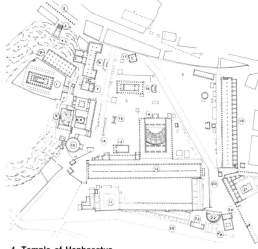

1 Temple of Hephaestus
2 Hellenistic Building
3 Sanctuary of Demos and Graces
4 Temple of Aphrodite Ourania
5 Stoa of early Roman date
6 Stoa of Zeus Eleutherios
7 Temple of Apollo Patroos
8 Metroon
9 Bouleuterion
10 Tholos
11 Heliaia
12 Middle Stoa
13 Roman Temple
14 Eponymous Heroes
15 Altar of Zeus Agoraios
16 Temple of Ares
17 Altar of 12 Gods
18 Odeion of Agrippa and Gymnasium
19 Stoa of Attalos
20 East Stoa
21 Library of Pantainos
22 Nimphaeum
23 Southeast Fountain
24 Southeast Temple
25 Mint
26 South Stoa

Agora: reconstruction of the south side, with Agrippa's Odeion

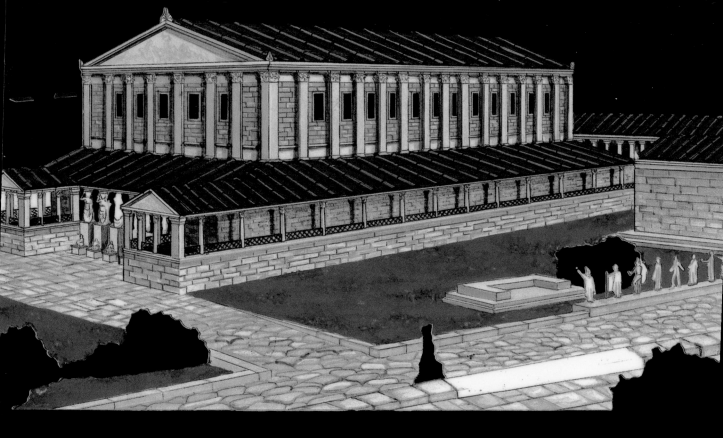

Hephaestus which, although it was devoted to Hephaestus and Athena, since the Middle Ages it has been called **Theseum**.

Thanks to a restoration before the seventh century AD and its conversion into a temple of Saint George in 1300, the Hepheasteum is preserved in excellent condition. In order to turn it into a temple of the Orthodox Christianity, they added an arch, filled the space between the pillars and opened several graves in the floor of the temple, which was housed under a dome. All these additions are today removed and the temple has its original shape. Its construction began in 448 BC, right after the peace treaty with Persia, following a plan similar to these of the temples of Poseidon in Sounio, of Nemesis in Rhamnous and of Ares in the attic borough of Acharnae, which was transported and rebuilt in the site of the Agora during the Roman period. All four temples are believed to have been constructed by the same architect, who remains unknown.

Athens. Hadrian's Arch

The temple of Hephaestus is a peripteral temple with six Doric pillars on the façades and thirteen on the long sides and is 100 attic feet long (32.77 metres). Each pillar is 5.88 metres high and has 20 deep grooves. The friezes had relief representations of a Centauromachia and of the apotheosis of Hercules, but are now lost. However, there are still preserved the ten metopes of the façade depicting the Labours of Hercules as well as the first four on each long side depicting the Labours of Theseus which probably accounts for re-naming the building at the

Middle Ages. Inside the Hephaesteum, the temple has two Doric pillars 5.38 metres high. In a completely innovative style, the architrave above the pillars was prolonged up to the outside pillars in such a way that it gracefully highlights the space between the front and the side pillars: it is thus a fore-room.

This new space's autonomy was emphasized by a metope above the architraves depicting scenes from the battles against the Cyclops and the Giants. Inside, the temple had on each of its three sides a two-storey row of Doric pillars, like the temple of the Parthenon. Here, there were the statues of Hephaestus and Athena, works of the great sculptor Alkamenes. Each side was to receive a coat of plastered gold, today lost. On the right side there are graves of victims of the liberating war of Greece, some of which are British and two Italians.

On the side of the Agora towards the hill of Theseum there are ruins of several public buildings of the fifth century BC. Among them, the most important are the Stoa of Zeus Eleutherios, defender of Freedom, the temple of Apollo Patroos, the Metroon, a peculiar building which housed the shrine of the Mother of the Gods as well as the state archives, the Bouleuterion, where the 500-member of the parliament met, and the round building called Tholos, where the Pritaneis came to eat and exercise their functions of government. Before the Metroon, on a long marble pedestal, there were the brass statues of the ten "eponymous" heroes, those who gave their names to the ten tribes of Attica. On the façade of this pedestal there were wooden boards where all the official laws and notices were displayed.

Directly in front of the temple of Apollo Patroos stand the foundations of the temple of Ares, built in the fifth century BC in Acharnae by the unknown architect of Theseum. After the orders by Augustus, the temple was transferred to the site of the Agora, as a symbol of victory.

The buildings at the far northern edge of the Agora are crossed by the rails of the Athens-Piraeus train. At this site, excavations have brought to light the *Basileios Stoa*, seat of the Archon, under whose chairmanship the council of Areopagus met to judge cases of homicide, arson and impiety. It was here that in 399 Socrates was tried. On the north side one can see the ruins of Heliaea, the official lay courts of Attica.

During the Hellenistic period, at the eastern and southern side of the Agora there were built three large two-storey porticos. From the south portico, possibly destined by the king of Egypt Ptolemaeus VI to be a gymnasium, only a few relics are left, upon which later a public baths complex was built. The eastern portico, which was built by the king of Pergamos Attalus II (159-138 BC) was remoulded with precision by the American School between 1953 and 1956 and today it dominates the Agora. The façade, restored with Pentelic marble, is 116.50 metres long and at the lower level it has 45 Doric pillars, whereas on the upper level there are 45 Ionic pillars. The interior, 19.40 metres deep, is divided into two parts by a row of 25 pillars along its length, of Ionic order at the lower level and of Corinthian order at the upper level. In 267 AD the Stoa of Attalus was set on fire by the Erouls and later its ruins were embodied to the new walls

The so-called "Tower of the Winds"

after Balerianus' orders. Thus, one can see today its form up to the second floor. The Stoa houses the Museum of the Agora , where one can see the excavation findings.

During the Roman period, the centre of the square occupied a grandiose building, the Odeion, built in 14 BC by Agrippa, Augustus son-in-law. It was a semicircle auditorium inside a square roofed building which had continuous two-storey roofed rows of pillars on each side. The Odeion was destroyed in 267 AD and upon its ruins was built around 400 AD the great gymnasium of the "Giants", named after the decoration of the propylon with the colossal statues of a Giant and two Tritons, still preserved today.

THE TEMPLE OF POSEIDON IN CAPE SOUNION

Detail from the bronze statue of Poseidon of Artemision (Nat. Arch. Museum)

Cape Sounion is one of the eastern edges of Attica, extending in the Aegean Sea. It is the first part of the attic land that one sees when coming from the Aegean islands or from the coasts of Minor Asia and the last that one leaves behind when departing from Athens. For that reason, from the ancient times, people built there a temple devoted to the god of sea, Poseidon. From the end of the seventh century BC and onwards, people started placing at the same spot colossal Kouroi (statues of young men) that can be found today in the National Archaeological Museum in Athens. In the beginning of the fifth century, at the cape's very edge, began the construction of an archaic temple made of poros stone. In 480 BC, before the work was completed, it was destroyed by the Persians.

In its place, between 445 and 440 BC a large Doric temple was built, of which today are preserved 15 pillars, 9 on the southern side and 6 on the northern. Initially, there were 6 pillars on the façades and 13 on the long sides and each one of them had 16 grooves only, in contrast with the usual form of 20 grooves. The interior of the temple had the typical tripartite arrangement, comprising a porch, a cella (central hall) and an opisthodrom (rear hall), but, like the Hephaesteum, the upper architrave was extended alongside the cella up to the exterior row of pillars. Thus the porch was adorned inside with an Ionic metope from marble of Paros with relief representations of the battles against the Amazons.

THE TEMPLE OF APHAEA IN AEGINA

Literally at the centre of the Saronic Gulf, between Athens, Corinth and Epidaurus, the small island of Aegina possesses one of the most unique natural locations in Greece. It has been inhabited since the Neolithic era, and a lot of material concerning the life and civilization of these first inhabitants are preserved until today. During the so-called Greek Middle Age the island remained deserted, but around 850 BC it was inhabited by Doric races coming from Epidaurus. In the seventh century BC Aegina was already one of the largest naval powers and we know that she was the first among the Greek cities that developed minting. As it was allied with Sparta and the other Peloponnesian cities, she has been for many years a great opponent of Athens at the naval field until two defeats and a capture of the city in 457 BC reduced her to a vassal to Athens.

During the period of its grandeur, the island, already reputed for its workshops of bronze, brass and pottery, was embellished with several Sanctuaries. The most famous is the sanctuary of Aphaea, a local goddess, related to the Cretan goddess Britomartis, who was later matched with Athena. On an imposing artificial balcony overlooking the entire Saronic Gulf, 12 miles away from the city, rose from the archaic period a sacred yard with a temple. Around 510 BC that temple was destroyed and was replaced by a new large Doric temple, one of the masterpieces of Greek Archaic architecture. It is a peripteral temple with six Doric pillars on each façade and twelve on each long side, made of local poros stone covered with marble plaster decorated with painted illustrations. At the interior, the porch and the opisthodrome had two pillars whereas the cella was divided into three naves with a double row of five pillars; above them, there was a second row of smaller pillars which supported the roof. The original multi-colority is lost. However, a large part of the pillars and parts of the architraves, the metopes and the walls of the cella were restored between 1956 and 1960. The holes between the pillars reveal the previous existence of railings.

The friezes were adorned with sculptures from Parian marble and are among the masterpieces of the Greek archaic art. These sculptured representations presented labours of the Aegean heroes, especially those of Aeas and his father, Telamonas during the Trojan War under the watchful eye of Athena. In 1811 they were discovered by Coquerel and were subsequently sold to Louis I of Bavaria, who ordered their restoration to the sculptor Thordvadsen. After this disastrous operation of the latter, they were exhibited to the Museum of Munich, where they remain until today. The remains of a third frieze came to light many years later, during the excavations at the sacred yard, and are kept today at the National Archaeological Museum in Athens. They are probably part of an older work that was destined for the eastern frieze, destroyed by the Persians in 490 BC and later exposed in memory of the Persian cruelty.

The Temple of Aphaea in Aegina: reconstruction

Corinth is built on the Isthmus, the canal connecting Central Greece with the Peloponnese; she overlooks the Saronic Gulf, the Aegean as well as the Ionian Sea protected by the hill of the Acrocorinth and possesses numerous springs. The city called by Homer Ephyra ("the richest") occupies one of the most privileged locations in continental Greece. For that reason, she was inhabited from the fifth millennium BC and had been the mythical city of Medea, of Sisyphus and of Vellelrephontes. She was re-established by the Dories and she was the first among the Greek cities where hereditary kingship evolved into aristocracy, under the rule of the Bachiadae dynasty and later into tyranny with Cypselus and Periandrus as the first tyrants (629-585 BC). At that time she was one of the biggest colonial powers, founder of Corfu and Syracuse, as well as one of the pioneers in the production of copper utensils and vessels, which were largely exported in all the markets of the Mediterranean between 650 and 550 BC. In Corinth, architecture was particularly advanced and it is alleged that the frieze was a Corinthian invention. Later, she was overshadowed by Athens, but

CORINTH

Corinth: View of the Temple of Apollo

excelled once again during the Hellenistic years as the centre of the fight against the Roman occupation. For this reason, in 146 BC, Consul Mommio pillaged her and annihilated her inhabitants.

Corinth remained deserted for a whole century, until Julius Caesar established here a colony of emancipated Romans, thus soon returning to her previous glory and becoming the capital of Roman Greece. Between 51 and 52 AD Apostle Paul lived and preached in Corinth. Although the city did not suffer the barbarian invasions that deserted the city of Athens, she gradually fell to a decline which reached its peak after the damages caused by the earthquakes of 522 and 551 AD; later, she played an important part due to the strategic position of her fort.

The city is built on a rocky hill above the Isthmus. Around 550 BC, on the most conspicuous position, they built **one of the most ancient Doric temples in Greece, devoted to Apollo**. This was a peripteral long temple with 6 pillars on the façades and 15 on each long side. A transversal wall divided the main temple into two sections. Each section had a

Corinth: The Peirene Fountain

façade with two pillars, a porch and a cella with a double row of pillars at the back.

The biggest part of the temple was destroyed, but one can follow its plan by the indentations on the walls used to insert plaques. Today, in their place, there are seven pillars on the south, over the Agora and on the east, above the road with the pillars that led to the port of Lechaeon. On the northwestern side one can see the two large theatres on the slope of the mountain, brought to light after excavations.

From the very ancient times, the **AGORA** constituted the centre of Corinthian life, although it was completed as late as the first century BC, during the restoration of the city by the Romans. The Agora looks like a large (160x95 metres) cobblestone square. It can be reached from the western side, passing from the Museum, where works of pottery and sculpture coming from the city and its outskirts are kept. Among other things, the Museum holds the statues of the family of Augustus, coming from Julia Basiliki and the relief decoration of the proscaenium of the Roman theatre built under Nero. On the western side of the Agora, the perspective was interrupted by a series of six small Roman temples and a circular monument with 8 Corinthian pillars, again from the Roman era, financed by the nobleman Babbius. On the northern side, there were a series of 15 workshops in front of which there was a row of Ionic pillars; above them rose the Temple of Apollo. In the central and largest shop a vaulted roof of the first century AD is preserved until today. On the eastern side, the series of the shops meets with the end of the façade of the Roman Basilica of the second century AD, in which there used to be the *Stoa Of the Slaves* as it was called thanks to the colossal statues of slaves made of Parian marble which were on the second floor, above a lower row of Corinthian pillars. Two of these statues can now be seen at the Museum of the Agora. This portico was built in front of the marble propylea, at the entrance of the Agora, where the Lachaion road ended. At the time Pausanias lived, the propylea's top was adorned with the gilded bronze chariots of Helios and his son Faethon. The road with the pillars leads to the Peribolos of Apollo (the sacred yard) and to the famous from the play *Medea* Peirene Fountain. This is an ancient natural spring inside a building first constructed on the sixth century BC but which was restored several times up to the Byzantine period. At present, there are preserved the great temple of the Nymphs and the three arches built under Herodes Atticus' orders the second century BC, in front of which there is a housed portico with three arcs. Inside the portico, the water from the spring is collected in four large tanks which are interconnected with underground channels.

On the eastern end of the Agora there are two large Roman buildings. One is Basilica Julia, with a quasi-prostylon bearing an arrangement of pillars on the top. The other was a Basilica with a prostylon and three naves. Before the Basilica Julia, at the site of the Roman square, excavations revealed the point of departure of running races which, according to Pindarus, were organized during the Ellotia, the festivals honoring Athena Elliotida.

On the south side, the Agora had two banks on whose façade there were shops. In the middle of the lower balcony, one can still see the Orato's Pedestal, from where Apostle Paul preached the words of the Lord before the Roman Consul (Apostles, 18). At the front of the upper bank there was a colossal housed portico with 71 Doric pillars on the façade and 34 Ionic ones inside which was constructed in the fourth century BC but was later restored by the Romans.

Reconstruction of the northwest corner of the Agora of Corinth

EPIDAURUS

In a green valley full of springs and streams, 10 kilometres on the west of the city of Epidaurus by the sea, the cult of the waters was practiced since the mycenaean times. We know that there used to be since the seventh century BC a Sanctuary of Apollo, earlier used for the worship of god-hero Maleatas. Later, to the cult of these two gods it was added a new divinity, related to the water, which might have arrived to Epidaurus from Thessaly: the cult of Asklepios. Whereas the worship of Apollo-Maleatas continued at a temple on the nearby mountain Kynortion, deep in the valley, near the sacred springs, a new Sanctuary was built especially for the worship of Asklepios. Soon the Sanctuary gained great importance and on the fourth century BC it was fully restored. At the same time, on the slope of the mountain northeast from the temple, a theatre was built, famous since that time for being the prettiest of all the Greek theatres; this theatre is still preserved in almost excellent condition.

THE THEATRE. The circular orchestra of 20.28 metres diameter has a centre altar of Dionysus (*thyméle*). A small ditch (*euripus*) runs around its perimeter, in order to collect the rainwater. The *cavea* has the shape of a fan, with 34 rows of seats, divided into 12 sectors by scales holding approximately 6200 spectators. Beyond the semicircular corridor (*diazoma*), at a later period, there were added 21 new rows of seats with a capacity of another 14000 spectators. The analogy between the number of rows of the upper and lower diazomae is considered to be mathematically "perfect". The first and the last row of the lower part and the first of the upper part had seats with backs and these seats were reserved for distinguished citizens.

A complicated set of relationships, largely based on the theory of the golden cut, gave the theatre ideal aesthetic harmony and almost perfect acoustics.

The stage that rose behind the orchestra, most of it lost, was supported by 12 Ionic pillars while at each end it had a jutting-out wing. However, during the Hellenistic as well as the Roman period, it underwent several changes that altered its original shape. As it usually happens in Greek theatres, the two spaces between the stage and the cavea (*parodoi* or passings) were left open to the public due to great circulation. These were adorned with two glorious entrances with Corinthian pillars.

Every year at this theatre there took place feasts in honour of Asklepios, including musical and dramatic presentations. In 1954 the theatre was restored into its original shape and since then it hosts every summer the productions of the Epidaurus festival.

The theatre of Epidaurus: reconstruction of the stage and part of the cavea

THE SANCTUARY OF ASKLEPIOS. Going downhill from the theatre and passing by the Museum, one can reach the Sanctuary.

On its right side there are the ruins of the *katagogeion*, a large square building built around 300 BC. It contained four yards surrounded with pillars and 160 rooms, used to host the pilgrims.

Further down there are the impressive remains of the gymnasium which contained a large yard with a housed portico. During the Roman period, at the centre of the yard there was constructed an Odeion. One can still clearly see the structures of the seats and the stage made of terra-cotta stone. At the same period, a temple devoted to goddess *Hygeia* (Health) was added near the entrance.

On the left side there is the stadion (181.10x21.51). The plaques marking the departure line are still preserved, as well as some of the seats. This stadion hosted the athletic competitions in honour of Asklepios.

The yard of the Sanctuary of Asklepios is found opposite another sports area of the Greek period, restored during the Roman era, and the remains of the foundations of a small pillared temple of goddess Artemis with four Doric pillars on the façade, dating from the fourth century BC.

Epidaurus, The Temple of Asklepios

Proposed reconstruction of the Tholos of Epidaurus

Architectural elements of the Tholos, Epidaurus, Museum

In the centre, there is an altar whereas on the western side there is the temple of the god. It was built on 380 BC by the architect Theodotus and was embellished with sculptures by Timotheus and Theotimus. It had six Doric pillars on the façade and 12 on each long side. Thus, it was a rather small temple and indeed, the cella had the usual porch but no opisthodrome. The friezes, some of which are kept in the National Archaeological Museum in Athens, depicted representations of an Amazonomachia and the capture of Troy. The caps of the long walls, the *acroteria*, were adorned with the sculptures of the goddess Hygeia and of two Nereids or Auras. The most celebrated building, however, the **Tholos**, on the west of the Temple of Asklepios, was built around 350 BC by Polykleitus the Younger and was so admired by Pausanias that he called it **Thyméle**. This was a circular building with 26 Doric pillars at the exterior of a circular cella; a second ring of 14 Corinthian pillars rose from within the cella. The roof had the form of a ring-shaped cone. The sculptures, part of which are kept in the local Museum, were very rich. Today, only the floor remains from the Tholos. There are still visible the foundations in concentric circles that meet with side corridors in such a way thus creating a sort of a labyrinth. One could enter from the centre of the Tholos through a spiral staircase, some of whose steps are still visible. It seems that this peculiar structure was connected with the cult of Asklepios. In order to obtain the oracles from the god, the priest had to go down in the Tholos' cellars, following a narrow spiral corridor that symbolized the descent to the depths of the earth.

While the two temples took up the centre of the yard, along its edges there were the most characteristic buildings devoted to curing. Before entering them, the patients had to wash in god's sacred springs. Thus, they had to participate in purifying ceremonies and to undergo fasting and other tasks defined by the priests. After being thus prepared, they were stretched at a special space, the Abaton or Enkoimeterion, where they would fall in deep sleep, during which often the god would appear in the shape of a snake. Then, he would either cure them himself, or he would give them a kind of medical advice which had to be interpreted by the priests. Often, the cure was achieved thanks to suggestion as well as thanks to the medical competence the priests of Asklepios had gained.

The *Enkoimeterion* is a long building on the northern side. It consists of a two storey housed portico with 34 pillars on the façade, which is 70 metres long. Its interior is divided into two parts which used to have settees. It was built on the fourth century BC but it used an underground gutter from the sixth century. On the eastern side there were found inscriptions of certain miraculous cures, today kept in the Museum.

The large space north of the Sanctuary of Asklepios is occupied by numerous offering monuments. Far back, one can see the ruins of a block of Curative Baths as well as other Roman buildings. By following the paved road, one reaches the place where there were the great gates of the Sanctuary, through which passed the Sacred Way commencing from Epidaurus. Today, only a few in-between parts of the stairs and the poros stone foundations remain.

Detail of the coffered ceiling of the external colonnade of the Tholos, Epidaurus, Museum

MYCENAE

The oldest archaeological findings from Mycenae are dated around 3000 BC. However, during the alleged Middle Helladic period (1900-1600 BC) the hill was fortified with walls and on the western side there was built a cemetery with tombs inserted in the rock. Around 1600 BC there were built much larger tombs, reserved for distinguished figures. At the same time, they started opening far from the city colossal vaulted tombs, consisting of a long entering corridor and a spacious circular room with a vaulted roof. During the Late Helladic period, the Mycenae were under the sphere of influence of Crete (1600-1500, First Late Helladic Period). Later, Mycenae developed their own civilization, the Mycenean, between 1500 and 1200 BC, which spread to the whole south of Greece, the Mediterranean coasts down to Syria and up to Italy. Around 1350 BC on the hill of Mycenae there were built new colossal walls, preserved up to the present, which surrounded among others a large number of Royal graves. This was the period of the climax of Mycenaean civilization which reached an abrupt end around 1200 BC after the city was abandoned. It seems that slightly earlier than 1100 BC the acropolis was destroyed, as the numerous signs of arson revealed by excavations indicate. Herein after, the place remained uninhabited for many years.

The traditions and legends of this heroic era not only have they been the most important source of intellect of Ancient Greeks but they have also inspired for many centuries the arts and literature of western civilization, from Aeschylus, Euripides and Sophocles to Shakespeare, Racine, Goethe, Vittorio Alfieri, Eugene O' Neal and Jean Paul Sartre.

Homer refers to Agamemnon, the king of Mycenae, as the commander of the Greeks in the Trojan War; he also mentions his brother Menelaus, who became king of Sparta after he married Helen, the daughter of the Spartan Tyndareus, who was kidnapped by Paris and was taken to Troy. It is believed that all these figures were related to the legendary war that marked the end of the VII phase of Troy which is located by archaeologists around 1240 BC, i.e. during the peak of Mycenaean power.

Mycenae. Gold Mask from Circle A (16th cent. BC)

Today Mycenae is one of the loveliest places in Greece, thanks both to its natural beauty as well as to the great charm of the archaeological site, associated with so many myths.

Gold rhyton in the form of a lion's head

Gold ring, diadem and goldcup from the Royal Graves at Mycenae

The Lion Gate

Grave Circle A

THE TREASURY OF ATREUS. The visit begins from the lower city, where the cemeteries are. The most distant cemetery is the most glorious one. This is the *Treasury* of Atreus, as the construction of the "tholos-tombs" was called in antiquity. A long corridor, the **dromos**, 36 metres long, partly cut into the rock and walled with conglomerate blocks of ashlar masonry leads to a gate 5.40 metres high, surmounted by a lintel and a relieving triangle. The lintel consists of two monolithic architraves, each one literary being a large block of stone, the largest weighing 118 tons. Once, the entrance must have been decorated with two small pillars covered with marble plaster which depicted multicoloured painted representations. Some fragments of these decorations are today kept in the British Museum in London.

The burial chamber or Tholos has a diameter of 14.50 metres and it is 13.20 metres high. It is housed by a vaulted roof formed by 33 superimposed courses of joined conglomerate blocks. The vault was adorned with copper rosettes, of which today only a few flowers and small nail holes are preserved. This was certainly a royal grave and it dates from 1330 BC. Therefore, it cannot belong to the victor of Troy VII or even to his father.

On the slopes of the same mountain there were discovered more similar graves, whereas a group of such graves is found near the walls of the city. Two of them were usually called the Tomb of Aegisthus and the Tomb of Clytemnestra. The first is one of the oldest of its kind and dates from about 1500 BC, whereas the second is believed to date from 1300 BC. This last tomb was built on an earlier group of royal graves, called Grave Circle B, which came to light by accident in 1951. In this circle, there were discovered 25 Shaft Graves with impressive funeral offerings made of gold and ivory, dating from about 1650 up to 1550 BC.

Mycenae. Gold and silver daggers from the Royal Graves

The Treasury of Atreus: reconstruction of the dromos and the façade

THE ACROPOLIS. Around the Acropolis rise the "cyclopean" walls, with roughly hewn limestone blocks. The length of these walls is 900 metres whereas their width is between 6 and 9 metres. Originally, their height must have reached in certain parts 19 metres. The visitor enters the fortified citadel through the **Lion Gate,** named after the relief plaque on the relieving triangle over the lintel, which depicts two lionesses facing each other; between them, there is a small pillar which, according to archaeologists depicts Authority. The Gate consists of four monolithic limestone plaques; two vertical embrasures, the threshold and the lintel. Next to the Gate, excavations brought to light the ruins of a granary with the signs of the 1100 BC arson still visible. Several large clay storage-jars still contained burnt wheat. At this spot the walls extended up to the older **Grave Circle A**, a circle of 28 metres diameter, enclosed by a double course of limestone slabs. Here, Eric Schliemann, between 1874 and 1876, discovered five large graves containing the remains of 19 skeletons and a large quantity of jewels and golden objects, among them the famous golden masks now kept in the National Archaeological Museum in Athens. Schliemann believed that he had found the graves of the Atreides. However, later, his findings were dated with greater precision from about 1600 and 1500 BC. Thus, all royal graves belong to the period of Mycenaean climax. The road continues in a spiral along the slopes of the mountain amid remains of Mycenaean houses, up to the royal palaces, which were built on the highest and most conspicuous spot. The buildings we see today were built after a part of the hill was leveled between 1400 and 1350 BC, on the ruins of an earlier palace, smaller in size, constructed around 1600 BC. Two quarters of the guard preceded a long corridor leading to the large yard. On the left side of the yard, there were the residential quarters. A small bath, plated with red marblestone, could be the bath in which, according to tradition, Clytemnestra slaughtered Agamemnon. On the right, a small staircase leads to the official quarters: a patio led to the hall of the throne, whereas a portico and a porch led to the most sacred place, the **Megaron** (Mansion). A circular hearth, plated with marblestone and decorated with painted representations stood at the centre of the hall. Four pillars, of which three bases are still preserved, supported the roof. Like in many contemporary palaces, the hall must have been decorated with painted stucco patterns. Even the floor was covered with coloured marblestone plaques, whose remains are there today.

The jar of the "Warriors" (c. 1200 BC)

Proposed reconstruction of the Megaron at Mycenae

A WALK AROUND THE ALTIS. One of the most important among the great sanctuaries of the religious and cultural life during the first centuries of Greek history is the sanctuary of Olympia. Allegedly, it was established by Pelops, the hero who gave his name to Peloponnese, but also by Hercules, who built the sanctuary in honour of Pelops himself or of Zeus. The place is mentioned as a place of worship since the beginning of the eighth century BC. This date corresponds with the date of the first athletic games, which are calculated to have taken place in 776 BC. These were sacred games that took place every four years during the August full moon and lasted for five days. All the cities and tribes of Greece participated in the games. Moreover, during the games, all the military activities and battles ceased. Their importance was so great that they constituted the basis for the Greek calendar system. The sanctuary of Olympia was famous both for its prestige as well as for its wealth and it never refrained from being embellished, especially during the sixth and fifth centuries BC. However, from the beginning of the Roman period, its decline started. In 86 BC Sylla pillaged it and in 80 BC he moved the Olympic Games to Rome. Along with the first emperors, Olympia experienced a new climax, until the end of the fourth century AD, when the orders of Theodosius outlawed all idolater acts thus marking the end of Olympia's peak.

OLYMPIA

Olympia, The Stadium

Proposed reconstruction of the Philippeion

THE PHILIPPEION. The sacred yard, called Altis, is inside a valley created by the river Alpheios and its tributary Kladeos, on the foot of mount Cronion. The priests came down here from the northwestern side, passing before the square building called Prytaneion.

In front of this building, Philip II of Macedonia built an impressive circular edifice, the Philippeion, in memory of the battle of Chaeronea in 338 BC. 18 Ionic pillars rose on a marble base and enclosed the wall of the cella, which was also circular, containing a ring of 9 small Corinthian pillars. This ring contained five chryselephantine statues of the Macedonian dynasty, a work of Leochares. These were the statues of Philip II himself, his parents Amyntas and Euridice, his wife Olympias and his son, Alexander the Great. The roof was decorated with marble tiles with palm-tree edges and gutters in the shape of lion heads. When Philip died in 336 BC, the temple was not completed and this task was undertaken by Alexander. The temple's rectangle yard was a place devoted to the worship of several divinities, probably the most ancient ones, such as Hera and Hippodameia on the female side and Pelops and Zeus on the male. Almost at the centre of the yard there was the **Pelopeion,** the burial of Pelops, the mythical king after whose name Peloponnese was named. Further north, near the slopes of Cronion, around 650 BC, the construction of a temple devoted to Hera began.

THE TEMPLE OF HERA. The original temple was a long and narrow hall 40x10 metres, with two pillars on the façade. The walls stood on a stone base of about one metre high, the vertical façade was made of terra-cotta stones and the roof was made of wood. Inside, a row of columns and pillars supported the walls on each side. Around 600 BC, the temple was restored with certain distinct renovations: on the back side, a symmetrical set of pillars was added. Furthermore, a ring of pillars, one of the first in Greece, enclosed the initial temple thus adding support to the roof. The first wooden pillars were substituted with stone. Even today, the visitor can detect the great differences in dimensions and art-form between the remaining pillars. During the second century AD, Pausanias recalls that the ancient temple of Hera preserved an oaken pillar. Initially, not just the drums, but also the capitals of the pillars must have been wooden. However, despite the perishable material used, the building was the first one possessing the form of the temple characteristic in the classical period. At the

Olympia. Detail from the Palaestra

Façade of the Heraion: reconstruction

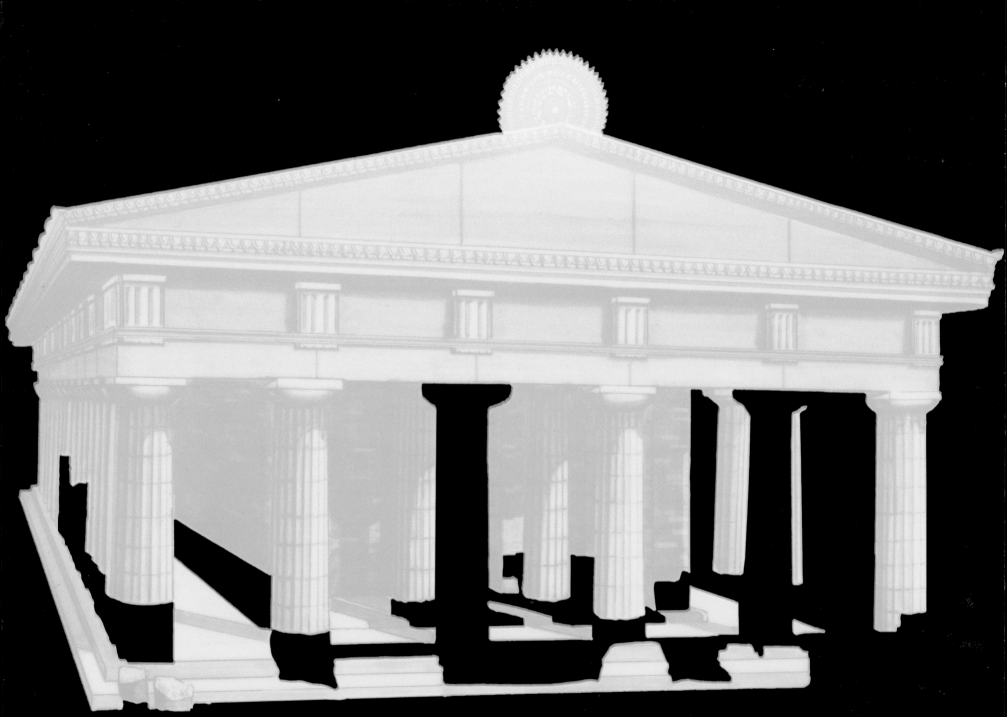

time when Pausanias wrote, the temple was converted into a kind of a Museum, carrying many masterpieces of sculpture. Among these, there is the marble Hermes of Praxiteles, found during excavations and kept in the Museum. The messenger of the gods is holding a young Dionysus in one hand, to whom he offers with the other raised hand, which is destroyed, a bunch of grapes.

THE TEMPLE OF ZEUS. As late as the fifth century BC was the greatest temple, devoted to Zeus, constructed. It is a work of the architect Libon of Elis and it was financed with the loot from the pillaging of the neighboring city of Pissa by the Eleans after 471 BC. Its construction was already completed when, in 456 BC, the Spartans deposited there a golden shield in memory of their victory in Tanagra.

The temple stood on a large three-level base which remains today intact and, it has been calculated, it was 200 Olympic feet long, i.e. 64.12 metres. The peripteral temple had 6 Doric pillars on the façades and 13 on each long side. Its total height was 20 metres. The main temple consists of the cella, the porch and the opisthodrome. The central space was divided into three naves by two rows of columns, each consisting of seven Doric columns on two levels. At the far end of the cella stood the enormous chryselephantine statue of Zeus, made by Phidias, which was considered one of the world's Seven Wonders. Just like the statue of Athena in the Parthenon, the bare members were ivory, while the clothes, hair and decorations were wood plated with gold. The god was depicted with a beard, sitting on his throne. On his left hand he held a large sceptre on the top of which an eagle stood, while on his right hand he held a sphere with a Nike. His legs were covered with a multi-pleated cloak, whose ends were lifted on one side to fall again on his left shoulder. Both the throne and the pedestal were adorned with elaborate relief representations. It is

The Hermes of Praxiteles

Inside view of the Temple of Zeus with the god's statue: reconstruction

believed that the statue was transferred to Constantinople during the fifth century AD, where it must have been destroyed in the 475 AD fire.

In front of the statue, according to Pausanias, there was a shallow basin with water so as to keep the necessary level of humidity in the room, in order for the ivory and the wooden skeleton of the statue not to wear out.

Between the pillars, there were railings adorned with mythological scenes by the painter Panaenos. However, the temple of Zeus was also decorated at the exterior. Two friezes, 12 metopes depicting

West pediment of the Temple of Zeus: a centaur grasps a Lapith woman

West pediment: detail of a young Lapith

the Labours of Hercules, the torsos of the lions on the gutters and 6 *acroteria* are preserved in good condition and are presently kept in the local Museum. These are masterpieces of the early period of classical art. The west frieze was decorated with relief representations of the battle between the Lapiths and the Centaurs, when the latter attempted to kidnap the former's women, whereas the centre is adorned with the grandiose statue of Apollo. The relief representations of the east frieze "narrate" the most ancient myth of Olympia: in the middle, there was the colossal statue of Zeus. On his right, there stood Oinomaos, the king of Pissa in Elis, who challenged into a chariot race the suitors of his daughter Hippodameia; he who would beat him, would marry her, whereas he who would lose, would die. On his left stood Pelops, the thirteenth and decisive suitor. Around them, there were Oinomaos' wife, Asterope and Hippodameia, slaves and chariots, as well as Oinomaos' driver, Myrtilos, who managed to overturn his master's chariot thus causing the latter's fatal fall. Finally, we see the personifications of the rivers of Olympia, Cladeos and Alpheios. In front of the two large temples, there stand today the numerous pedestals of the offering statues. These were placed in order to honour the victors in the games, the Olympic victors. Allegedly, in the era of Plinius the Senior (first century AD), they were 3000! Many of them are described in detail by Pausanias on the 2nd century AD and are identified by their signed bases. Some of them had been embodied in the Byzantine walls. Moreover, there have been identified the bases of the chariots of the tyrants of Syracuse, Gelon and Ieron as well as the high triangular pilaster on top of which stood the statue Nike, a masterpiece by Paionios. The pieces of the statue have been reconstructed and it is kept today in the Museum of Olympia.

On its north side, the sacred yard of Altis reaches the slope of Cronion. Here excavations revealed a long terrace on which there stood the *thesauroi* (treasures), a kind of small temples the largest cities of the sixth and fifth century BC used to build, in order to install inside their offerings. There is the small temple of Gela, on the eastern edge of the terrace which is also the oldest and largest, built around 600 BC, that of Megara, of Metapontion, of Selenous, of Cyrene, of Sibare, of Byzantium, of Epidamnos, of Syracuse and of Sykion. At the base of the terrace there stood 17 statues of Zeus; these were installed there by offenders as a plead for forgiveness, a law enforced by the lords of Olympia.

West pediment of the Temple of Zeus: god Apollo

East pediment of the Temple of Zeus: the old seer

THE NYMPHAEUM OF HERODES ATTICUS.

On the west end of the terrace, opposite the temple of Hera, around 150 AD, Herodes Atticus financed the construction of a large Nymphaeum. Since water in Olympia is scarce, the water coming from the mountain was channeled into underground aqueducts. The nymphaeum consisted of a large, semicircular reservoir, enclosed by double rows of pillars in perspective. In between the pillars, there were niches adorned with statues, carrying two statues of Zeus, as well as the statues of the imperial family and the family of Herodes, joined by that of Anna Regilla, to whom the Nymphaeum was dedicated.

West pediment:
the centaur Eurytion and Deidameia

The façade of the reservoir was adorned with gutters in the shape of lion heads, together with a marble bull with a signed base. At the building's sides stood two round pavilions. A large part of the statues and the rest of the decoration were found during excavations and are kept in the Museum together with other statues, mainly of Roman emperors, found in the Metroon before the terrace. The Metroon is a small temple built during the fourth century AD in honour of the Mother Goddess and at the time of Augustus' rule, it became devoted to the cult of emperors.

On the east side, the sanctuary ended in a long and narrow portico built on the fifth century and restored on the fourth. It is called Echo Portico, because of the echo one could hear seven times over; it was also

The Nymphaeum of Herodes Atticus: reconstruction

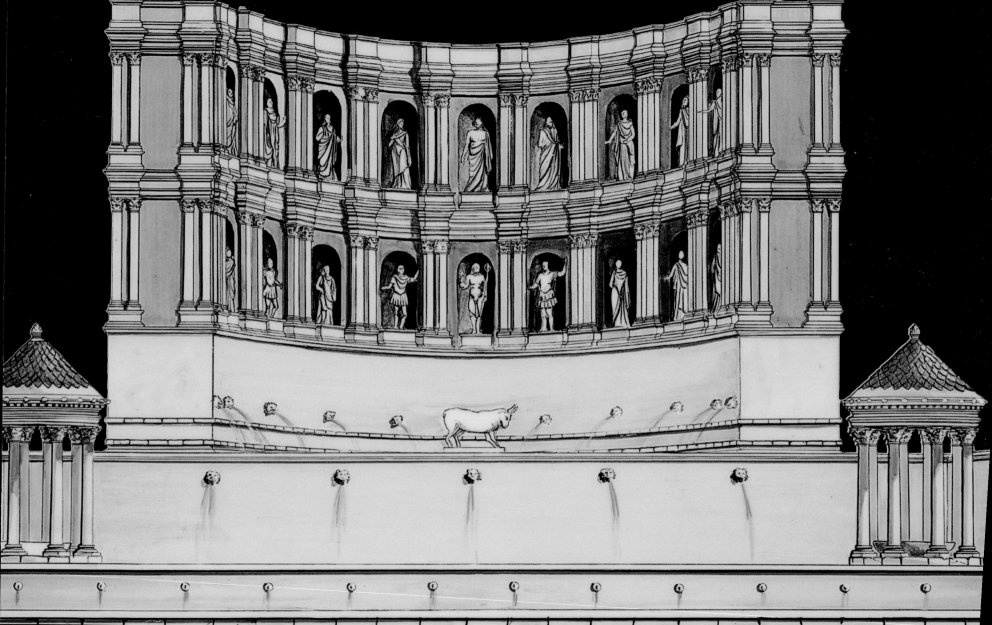

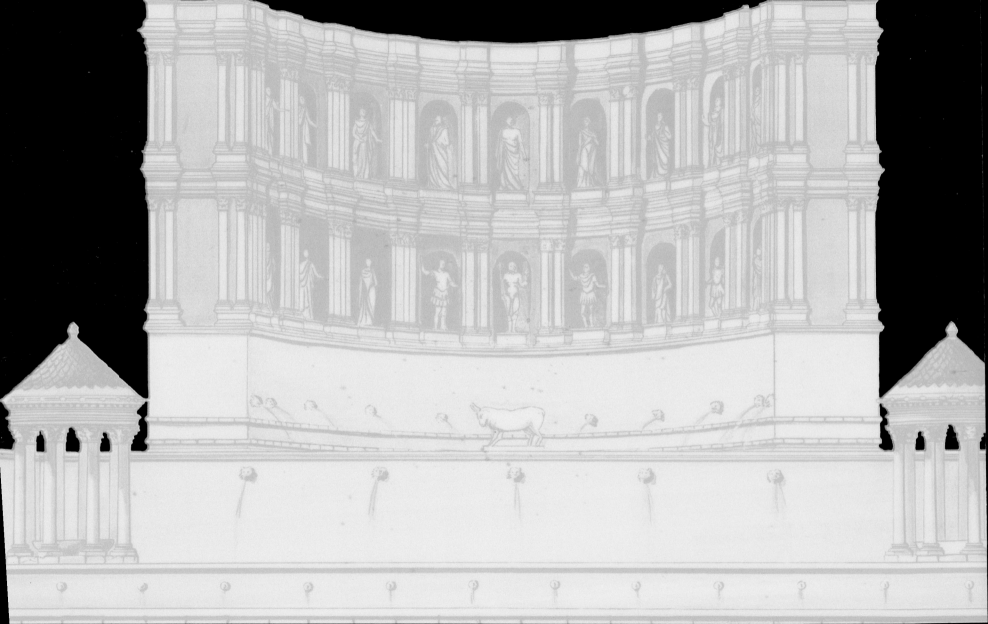

called *poikile* (painted), because it was decorated with paintings.

This portico separates the most sacred place, the **stadion**, which could be reached through a narrow corridor between this portico and the terrace of thesauroi. In this stadium, the most celebrated games in history took place every four years. Today there are clearly visible the start and finish lines with a 600 Olympic feet distance between them; thus, a *stadion* measured 192.27 metres. The space was enclosed with an artificial bank, on which the spectators would watch the games and which could seat 40000 people. Several other buildings were constructed during antiquity around the sacred yard of Altis, which were related to the games and life in the sanctuary. Along the river Cladeos there are the ruins of a large rectangle **gymnasium** and of a **palaestra** with a large yard enclosed by 19 Doric pillars on each side; its interior possessed many spaces with Ionic and Corinthian rows of pillars. This palaestra was built on the third century BC to host the gymnastic games. Further south, almost opposite the temple of Zeus, excavations brought to life a block of buildings of rare significance. Indeed, besides the private apartments of the priests, this block included a large space with three parts, which in terms of its orientation and dimensions was a perfect duplicate of the temple of Zeus. This was the **workshop of Phidias**, described in detail by Pausanias, where the great sculptor created the chryselephantine statue of the larger temple. The 1958 excavations brought to light, among others, an *"oinochoe"*, a pitcher with the inscription *"I belong to Phidias"*.

The Byzantine church built on the ruins of the workshop of Phidias

The Nike of Paionios. Museum of Olympia

DELPHI

The Sanctuary of Apollo in Delphi had been one of the most glorious oracles in antiquity, along with these of Zeus in Olympia and of Apollo in Delos. It is situated on the slope of Mount Parnassus, above the valley of Plisto. It was built during the archaic period to host the cult of the snake Python, son of Mother Earth. The place took its contemporary name when the cult of Apollo Delphinios, i.e. the god worshipped in the shape of a dolphin. Only very few elements of this cult survived. Even the priestess who delivered the oracles preserved the ancient name *Pythia*, whereas later she was also referred to as Sibyl. The sanctuary soon gained political importance, as it became the seat of one of the mightiest *amphictyoniae*, or holy alliances, and an essential reference point for all the Greek cities wishing to establish colonies on western Europe. It was honoured even by Kroisos, the extremely rich king of Lydia, as well as by the Pharaoh of Egypt Amasis. The sanctuary has been the cause of many sacred wars for its control, but its prestige remained intact. When in 373 BC it suffered serious damages by an earthquake, many city-states collaborated in order to restore it. During the Roman period it was honoured by the first Roman leaders and later by emperors such as Augustus, Nero and Hadrian. Gradually, however, it fell in decline. In 385 AD Theodosius outlawed paganism and forbade the existence of oracles. Since then , "the voice of the water faded away", as its last priests allegedly have said.

In contemporary times, the excavations at the archaeological site began in 1892 by a group of French archaeologists and are still under way.

THE TEMENOS OF ATHENA PRONAIA. Between two tall rocky hillsides of Parnassus, the *Phaedriads* ("shiny"- due to the shiny reflection of the sun on the rocks), still flow the waters of the Castalian Spring, which used to be the sacred Spring of the god and was adorned with a façade of bronze lion heads. From this spot, the archaeological site escalates upwards towards the east, while it descends towards the west. Upon one of the banks, called *Marmaria* as it was converted into a marble mine by the end of antiquity, there stood the temenos of Athena Pronaia. There is a series of the remains of five buildings devoted to religious practices. The ancient temenos of Athena, a peripteral temple with 6 Doric pillars on each façade was built of poros stone in the beginning of the fifth century BC in the place of a much more ancient temple. One can see the two *treasuries* of Massalia, which are small offering temples, the first dating from 490-460 BC and the second from 530 BC. Finally, one reaches the ruins of a large circular building, the **Tholos.** This is a circular platform on which there stood a ring of 20 thin Doric pillars, while inside the also circular cella there were 9 Corinthian pilasters incorporated in the walls. The general structure of the temenos is still visible today. Three external pillars together with their entablatures were restored in 1938. The building was made of Pentelic marble, charmingly matched with black poros stone, the latter used for the base of the cella's walls and the floor, except of the main round floor, which was also made of white marble. The vaulted roof was also elaborately decorated.

The Tholos was built in the beginning of the fourth century BC by the architect Theodoros of Samos. This masterpiece was an exemplary building, autonomous and in perfect harmony with the space. Its novelty so impressed the ancient people, that they soon imitated it in the *Thyméle* of Epidaurus and the Philippeion of Olympia.

The later temenos of Athena Pronaea sharply contrasted with the innovative frame of Tholos. The temenos, found on the eastern side of the Tholos, is a Doric building with 6 pillars on the façade and it was built around 360 BC upon earlier residents of priests.

On the banks between Marmaria and the Castalian Spring there were several buildings, among which a colossal gymnasium of the fourth century BC.

The largest sanctuary with the oracle of Apollo Pythios is on the West side. It consists of a large rectangle yard on the flattened part of a steep downward slope. The Sacred Way led to the sanctuary from the northeastern side and went up spirally to the temple of Apollo, between the *treasuries* and the other offering buildings. Right after the entrance stood the bronze bull, a work of Theopropos of Aegina; this was an offering from the people of Corfu in 480 BC after a successful fishing. We can still see its base today. On the left side, on a long platform, there stood the 16 statues of Phidias, dedicated by the Athenians in honour of the victor Miltiades, thirty years after the battle of Marathon (450 BC). Probably the two bronze statues found near Ryakis came from this monument.

Delphi.
The Treasury of the Athenians

Before this offering monument, the Spartans, after they humiliated Athens in the Peloponnesian War, built another monument, even more grandiose, the so-called Admirals' offering, with 37 bronze statues of gods and Spartan admirals and generals, including the statue of the victor of the battle at Aegos Potamous in 404 BC, Lyssandros. There are two more semicircle platforms, on which stood statues dedicated by the people of Argos to their kings, as well as other offering monuments, described in detail by Pausanias. At the flat area between the Sacred Way and the south part of the sanctuary's yard there stand today the remains

Delphi. Reconstruction of the Tholos of Marmaria

of three small temples, the *treasuries* of the Siphnians, the Sicyonians and the Athenians. The treasury of the Siphnians, which was built between 526-525 BC and financed by the island's gold mines, was a small temple of Ionic order with two Caryatids instead of pillars and a continuous long frieze of Parian marble 65 centimetres high which extended in all four sides. Today, this frieze is kept at the Delphi Museum and is one of the greatest masterpieces of the Archaic sculpture. At the façade, the frieze depicted myths from the capture of Troy. At the southern façade there was a relief representation of the kidnapping of the Leukippids. At the north and most conspicuous side, there was depicted the famous Gigantomachia. At the pediments, sculptures represented a very popular theme in attic pottery at the time. This is the confrontation between Hercules and Apollo for the sacred tripod, with Athena in the middle trying to separate them. The characteristic Ionic grace of this jewel was indeed very much opposed to the strict Doric order of the *Treasuries*. After the next turn of the road, we find ourselves in front of another treasury built by the Athenians right after 490 BC with the loot from the battle of Marathon. The building, restored in 1904-1906, resembles of a small Doric temple 9.70x6.70. It is adorned with a Doric frieze with characteristically alternate triglyphs and relief metopes. The works on the frieze seen today are copies, since the originals are kept in the Delphi Museum. To the mythical labours of Hercules there have been added the labours of Theseus, the original Athenian hero. The archaeologists believe that the pediment included a statue of Apollo. The walls carry more than 150 inscriptions, among which the resolutions favourable to Athens and two hymns to Apollo, containing between the verses some music symbols of the ancient people.

In front of this temple, after the unsuccessful expedition of Athenians to Sicily between 415 and 413 BC, the Syracuseans built their own treasury, of which only very few traces remain today.

Delphi. The Castalian Spring

THE TEMPLE OF APOLLO. The Sacred Way runs along the protective wall of the platform of the Temple of Apollo, which in the ancient times covered an Ionic row of columns made of Parian marble, financed by the Athenians after the Persian wars had ended. The platform before the temple was also filled with offerings. Among others, there stood the tripods submitted by the tyrants of Syracuse Gelon and Ieron after the victory in Imera (480 BC) against the Carchedonians, as well as the golden tripod with a cauldron which was supported by a bronze column with the shape of three winded snakes; these were offerings of the same period by the people of Plataeae. During the Christian era, this tripod was transported to Constantinople and its base still stands at the Cyan Temenos square.

On the platform, during the seventh century BC a temple was built, which was later destroyed in a fire in 548 BC. Around the end of the sixth century BC it was replaced by a new temple financed by the expatriate Athenian family of Alkmeonidae. When this building was in its turn destroyed, in 373 BC, it was rebuilt by

Delphi. Reconstruction of the Temple of Apollo

the architects Xenodoros and Agathon, who kept the same plans. What we have today is the result of all these restorations which took place between 1939-1941. The foundations of the pillars and the walls of the cella are still clearly visible, laid like two rectangles, one into the other.

It is a petipteral temple of Doric order, 60.32x23.82 metres, with poros stone pillars plated with marblestone, 6 on the small sides and 15 on the large ones. The cella had two pillars, both on the porch as well as on the opisthodrome, whereas inside there was the *adyton*, the most sacred of all spaces that no one could enter, since it contained the *omphalos*, the centre of the world. The pillars' architraves were adorned with the shields of Persians from the battle at Plataeae and of the Gauls of the third century BC. The roof was covered with marble tiles. It is believed that there was an underground space where only the pythian soothsayer could enter, in order to obtain the oracles from the gods.

The side of the platform close to the mountain, on the temple's right side, suffered serious landslides. During one of them, probably in 373 BC, the bronze chariot dedicated in 474 BC by the tyrant of Syracuse Polyzalos was buried. The statue of the Charioteer, in natural dimensions, is one of the most famous masterpieces of archaic art and was brought to light during excavations; today, it adorns the Delphi Museum.

A small scale connected this platform with the theatre, which was built on the fourth century BC and was restored during the Hellenistic and the Roman period. A terrace wall called *Ischegaon* from the verb *ischo* which means "to retain the earth" supported the cavea on the hillside. The cavea consisted of 35 rows of seats and had a capacity of 5000 spectators. One can still see the cobblestone orchestra and the foundations of the stage, adorned with a marble frieze depicting the Labours of Hercules, today kept in the Museum.

On the upper part of the yard there are the foundations of a building. Two rows of pillars divide its interior into three sectors. This is the Lesche of the Cnidians, which was built during the fifth century BC and gained fame thanks to the magnificent paintings of Polygnotos.

Above the sacred yard, a clear path leads to a small valley where the stadium is. A part of it was built during the fifth century BC, but it was subsequently restored several times. On the north side, towards the mountain, there are 12 rows of columns carved in the rock. On the opposite side, another 6 rows stand upon earlier foundations.

In this stadium there took place every four years the Pythian Games, which once again included musical and theatrical competitions, held at the theatre, as well as chariot races, held at the valley. In 528, right after the sacred war, the Pythian Games were reorganized with a new set of rules. Thereafter, they were taking place more often and went on until the end of antiquity.

Delphi. The Theatre

Delphi, Theatre, reconstruction of the stage

STOA OF THE ATHENIANS. The area of the *temenos* of the sanctuary is crossed by the **Sacred Way**, which winds its way up three ramps to reach the Temple of Apollo. The Sacred Way is lined with the treasuries (*thesauroi*) and votive monuments built by various cities in honour of Apollo.

The description of the Greek writer Pausanias, who visited the site in AD 160 and wrote an impressive ten-volume account of his travels "*A Periegesis (or Itinerary) of Greece*", is an invaluable aid for identifying the sanctuary's monuments.

On the left of the Sacred Way stand the ruins of what is known as the "monument of Athenian naval power": the **Stoa of the Athenians**. This Ionic stoa is 30 metres long and stands on a crepidoma, with 7 Ionic Parian marble columns along the front. The monumental inscription carved on the stylobate announces that the building was erected (after 478 BC) to house the trophies of the Athenians' naval victories over the Persians, including the rostra (prows of enemy ships) and the cables taken from the pontoon bridge built over the Hellespont by the Persian king Xerxes. Following the foundation of the stoa, the Athenians continued to use it to house their battle spoils and public resolutions were carved on the back wall of the structure.

Delphi, Stoa of the Athenians and south side of Apollo's Temple, reconstruction

Delphi, Sacred Way: bases of votive monuments; in the background the Treasure of Athenians

Another famous sanctuary is literally in the middle of the Aegean: this is the sanctuary of Apollo in Delos. The island was inhabited as early as from the third millennium BC and later, it passed under the sphere of influence of Naxos, the largest island of Cyclads. Since the Archaic period it was the most important religious centre in the Aegean, which in 477 BC it became the headquarters of the first Athenian alliance. In 454 BC, Pericles moved the treasury of the alliance to Athens and in 426 BC a purification of the island was ordered; it was thus forbidden to anyone to be born or die there. Thanks to her position, Delos enjoyed a great economic peak during the Hellenistic years. After the battle of Pydna in 168 BC, the Romans declared it a free port. This marked the beginning of a century of great affluence, which ended, however, with the destruction caused by the Mithridatean war, between 88 and 69 BC.

In antiquity it was believed that in Delos there was the sacred lake near which Lyto, hiding from the rage of Hera, gave birth to the twin divinities, Apollo and Artemis. Today, this lake does not exist anymore, but a stone yard marks its perimeter. At its centre a palm-tree was planted, in memory of the one under which, according to Homer, the two gods were born.

The excavations began in the last century by a French delegation and still continue.

During the seventh century BC, on a conspicuous spot above the lake, a platform was built, adorned with 9 archaic lions with extended bodies. Five of them are still preserved in their places. One was taken by Morosini to Venice and in 1962 he placed it in front of the Naval Station.

Further south there was the sanctuary of Apollo within the sacred yard. In the middle, there was the peripteral temple of the god with 6 Doric pillars on the façade and 13 on each long side; the temple was rather small (29.50x13.55). Its construction began soon after the establishment of the first Athenian alliance in 477 BC, but it was not completed in 454 BC when the treasury of the alliance was moved to Athens and it was thus left unfinished. Around the sanctuary of Apollo there are the foundations of several buildings, especially of *treasuries* and housed porticos. Both the zone of the lake, as well as the area around the sanctuary, which are considered to be among the most important archaeological sites in Greece, have been thoroughly excavated. Thus, there were brought to light the port along with a large number of shops and workshops, an entire neighborhood on the hillside, a theatre and the platforms of the eastern sanctuaries, on Mount Kynthos. The residences are dated from the golden Hellenistic century of Delos, between 168 and 69 BC and present great interest to the study of Greek houses. All the residences are found around a central yard, often decorated with a series of pillars, and consist of many storeys, as to harmonize with the slope. Their perimeter is often irregular; the road system is also irregular, as it was developed in a free manner, due to the influx of rich merchants from all parts of the Mediterranean, especially from Italy and Syria. Often, inscriptions have helped archaeologists obtain precise information about the proprietors. A very characteristic case was the one of a **residence near the theatre**, in which the statues of the owners were

DELOS

Delos. Reconstruction of the portico of the "House of Cleopatra"

found. Their inscriptions bear the date 138/7 BC and mention the names Cleopatra and Dioskourides, two rich bourgeois who moved to Delos from Athens. Today, at the portico there are two copies of the statues, while the originals, carrying the typical Hellenistic clear pleats of the clothes are kept in the Museum.

Delos. The procession way with archaic lions

CRETE

A concise reference to classical and pro-classical Greece could not be complete without at least a brief mention of Crete. Here, between 2500 and 1100 BC grew one of the greatest civilizations in the Mediterranean. One can visit some of the most impressive buildings of the copper period in Phaestos, Zakros, Mallia, Knossos and elsewhere.

THE PALACES OF KNOSSOS are certainly the most interesting and rich in archaeological findings. In here the mythical king Minos lived and ordered Daedalus to build the Labyrinth in order to confine the

Minotaur. With the help of Ariadne, Minos' daughter, Theseus managed to kill the beast. Inside the Labyrinth, Minos had imprisoned Daedalus himself together with his son Ikarus in order to punish them; however, they managed to escape by flying with wings they had made of wax.

The excavations which began around 199 by A. Evans have brought to light the signs of an earlier palace, built around 2000 BC, which around 1700 BC collapsed after an earthquake. A second, larger palace was built on its ruins, but this one as well collapsed around 1400 BC due to a new earthquake. Later, only a few residences were restored and inhabited again, which were at last abandoned around 1000 BC. The grandiose remains of the second palace, which was completed at the climax of the Cretan power (1600-1400 BC) are on a short hill at the top of an archaeological site. From the exterior, their façades do not seem straight, but they are full of indentations and protrusions, characteristic of the Minoan architecture.

The visitor enters the palaces from a magnificent gate with a pillar in the middle, and crosses a narrow corridor, the so-called *Corridor of the Procession* which was adorned with large frescoes of a procession, currently kept in the Museum of Herakleion. This corridor leads to a series of porticos, which in their turn lead to the staircase of the upper level, restored by Evans. At the other end, the corridor meets the large main yard, around which there are the palatial buildings. On the west side there are the Reception Halls, the tripartite shrine and the throne room which was built around 1450 BC. Inside, the alabaster throne is preserved, while the original frescoes have been restored; these frescoes depict facing hunchbacks and naturalistic motifs of extreme elegance. Opposite the throne room there are 22 palatial workshops. In the middle of the east side of the yard, a corridor leads to the spacious private quarters. The hall with columns serves as a porch. Going north, one reaches the quarters of the craftsmen and the Lapidary's workshop. On the south side there are the royal chambers; the room of the Double Axes, consisting of three porticos and several sources of light and the Queen's *Megaron,* whose entrance is decorated with a copy of the authentic fresco of dolphins, pieces of which were discovered in this room. On the west side of the room there was a bathroom. Moreover, there are three other spaces, probably serving as administrative headquarters. In one of them, there were discovered plaques with Linear B, a form of writing particularly rare in Crete (where Linear A was mostly used), more common at the Mycenaean centres.

On the north side of the main yard there is a long corridor that leads to a large room supported by a double row of pillars, which is called **Treasure House**, while nearby there is the north propylon, where another clay plaque with Linear B was found. On a short wall one can see the famous pillar crypt, restored by Evans, decorated with a copy of the fresco of the bull, the symbol of the Minoan power. The treasures kept in the National Archaeological Museum of Athens and the Museum of Herakleion reveal the high level of civilization the inhabitants of these palaces had achieved.

Jar decorated with flowers, from the palace of Phaestos. Crete, Museum of Herakleion

Minoan vessel with marine representations (c. 1450 BC)

SOUTH PROPYLAEUM. The West Court is paved and has causeways for processions. The three stone built pits ("kouloures"), are thought to have been used as rubbish pits for discarded sacred objects or as depositories in some phase; the two Altars were built in the last phase of the palaces.

A causeway leads from the Court to the West Porch which may have been where the king himself received foreigners. A double door opened into the Corridor of the Procession, so called because of the long procession of men and women gift-bearers painted on the walls. The Corridor, interrupted today on the south, originally led to the Southwest Entrance, at which an imposing Stepped Portico ended. Further south is the South House, which belonged to the high priest. The Corridor of the Procession turns eastwards and leads towards the South Propylaeum, where the procession ends (this was where the splendid fresco of the Rhyton Bearer was found).

Another approach to the Palace is by the South Porch, which leads into the north-south corridors and from them into the Central Court. Near Corridor were found the remains of the Prince of the Lilies.

The **Central Court**, into which Corridors lead, was the heart of the political, religious and economic life of the Palace. From the Corridor of the Procession a *polythyron* (partition of pier-and-doors) opens into the **South Propylaeum**. Here, in the Neopalatial period, as we have said, the Procession of approximately 500 giftbearers, including the Cup-bearer, ended.

Knossos, the "Rhyton Bearer", detail from the Procession fresco

The " Prince of Lilies" priest king, fresco detail

Knossos, the South Propylaeum of the Palace, reconstruction

THRONE ROOM. An imposing Staircase flanked by porticoes ascended from the South Propylaeum. A rectangular building to the right of the staircase is thought to have been a Greek Temple of Rhea, which we know from Diodorus to have existed ad Knossos.

The same Staircase leads to the Tricolumnar Shrine, which is just as it is depicted in the frescoes. It was decorated with a fresco of a sacred marriage.

Behind the shrine and exactly over the West Magazines is the Great Hall used for large gatherings, and to the north of it the Sanctuary Hall, where the famous fresco of the "Parisienne" was found. A light-well above the Throne Room comes out on a terrace, where copies of the frescoes are displayed. A staircase at the north end of the terrace leads to the groundfloor.

On the groundfloor are the Ante-room and **Throne Room**. The Ante-room is entered through a set of four piers-and-doors. On the north side of the Throne Room is the gypsum throne with a bench on either side, and behind the throne a pair of griffins, its guardians.

The sacred character of the room is evident from the "lustral basin" opposite the throne.

The squat alabastron-type of vases found on the floor show that a ceremony to propitiate the deity was in progress at the moment of the destruction.

There is a Stepped Porch south of the Throne Room with 12 steps and two columns in line on the steps to support the roof. South of and lower than the Stepped Porch, Cist-shaped Crypts lined with lead were found, which contained the faïence snake goddesses. These were the **Temple Repositories**. Directly south of the Stepped Porch the **Tripartite Shrine** fronts onto the Great Court. This type of shrine is well-known from the miniature frescoes.

It is shallow in depth. A fine large *pithos* is preserved behind its west wall. South of the Tripartite Shrine steps lead down to a paved area which was the Ante-room of the Pillar Crypt, a hypostyle chamber where sacrifices took place. The pillars, with double-axes carved on them, have the character of "baetyls", sacred stones that were abstract representations of the deity. Behind these compartments, on the other side of the long corridor, are the 18 West Magazines.

The "Parisienne", detail of a wall painting (Museum of Herakleion)

Knossos, reconstruction of the Throne Room

QUEEN'S MEGARON. The East wing had four floors, which are not entirely visible from the Central Court. The **Grand Staircase**, which had a protective parapet of panels and was illuminated by a light-well, was the principle entrance to the East Apartments. The Staircase and a corridor lead to the **Room of the Double Axes**, named after the symbol incised on its walls, which formed part of the King's Megaron.

Remains of an imposing throne made of gypsum were found in the room. Two sets of doors-and-piers opened onto it from the east, with a room between them used for audiences.

The doors-and piers were closed with wood or fabric. A small door and a dog's-leg corridor lead to the **Queen's Megaron**. The room has a double window and a door leading into a covered area with two doors and two light-wells. Fine frescoes were found in the Megaron, restorations of which are on the walls. The Dolphin fresco is on the north wall, and the "Dancer" fresco was found on a pilaster of the east set of doors-and-piers. West of the Megaron is the Queen's Bathroom, with a sit-bath, and the Toilet Room with a low bench and a lavatory. A door in the north wall of the Toilet Room leads into the **Court of the Distaffs**, called after the distaffs incised on the walls. In this courtyard and the lavatory one can see the wonderful plumbing system with cisterns and built drains. The small room behind the lavatory was the **Treasury**, in which many precious objects of gold, ivory, faïence and jasper were found; the famous Ivory Bull-leaper was found here under a small stone staircase.

Other rooms in the area south of the King's and the Queen's Megarons that are worth visiting are the **Shrine of the Double Axes**, in which cult figurines of the Mycenaean period with their hands raised were found on a ledge.

Further south are private dwellings, like the Southeast House, where a metal furnace was found, the House of the Sacred Chancel, the House of the Sacrificed Oxen, the House of the Fallen Blocks, all named after the finds in them. Outside the area of the site is the Minoan guest house, the Caravanserai, and further south again on the Knossos-Archanes road, the two-storey South Royal Tomb. From the corridor that runs south of the King's Megaron another corridor leads to the Lapidary's Workshop, where many half-finished works were found. A room with benches to the north of this was called the Schoolroom, but it is more likely to have been a Potter's Workshop. Further north again, a door opens into the Court of the Stone Spout, which got its name from the long stone drain. The Toreador Fresco was found here. A little higher up is the Magazine of the Giant Pithoi which contains the largest pithoi found to date; south of it is the Southeast Bastion. Here you can see the drainage system beside the staircase. To the east, on the upper floor, is the large hall known as the East Hall. From this hall came the remains of a colossal wooden statue (it is estimated to have been 2.80 m high), whose bronze locks of hair have survived.

After the Magazine of the Giant Pithoi you come to the Corridor of the Draught-board, whose name comes from the

Knossos, the Queen's Megaron, reconstruction

royal game, a kind of chess-board made from ivory and other precious materials. Further to the southwest is the Magazine of Medallion Pithoi.

NORTH WING OF THE PALACE. From about the middle of the Central Court a corridor sloping northwards leads to the North Entrance, below which runs the central drainage conduit. On either side are covered hypostyle areas, the Bastions, which have masons' marks cut on their walls. A replica of the fresco of the Bull in an Olive Grove has been placed in the west one. A large pillared hall begins at the north end of the corridor, whose roof is supported by eight pillars and two columns, the so-called **Customs House**.

On the left is the North Entrance and Bastion that formed the main entrance. Besides this entrance, there was another, that must have been cultic in character, since it was next to a **Lustral Basin**. In the northwest corner a lid was fund with the name of the Pharaoh Khyan.

Northwest of the Central Court there is a building complex with rounded corners that belongs to the Prepalatial period (3ʳᵈ millennium BC), and below it Neolithic remains were found (6ᵗʰ millennium). Evans called this the Dungeons. In the last period of the Palaces a shrine was built on this spot, from the upper floor of which the Miniature Frescoes with the Tripartite Shrine, Sacred Grove and Blue Monkey Saffron Gatherer had fallen. In the northwest part of the Palace is the **Theatre Area**. The tiers of seats form an angle. A stone platform at the south corner is thought to have been the Royal Box. The two wings of seats are estimated to have seated 500 spectators. The area for the performances was low and stone paved, and there was a Processional Way with branches off it. The Processional Way met the Royal Road. There were houses on both sides of the road, like the House of the Frescoes and the Arsenal. Further to the west is the NW Treasure House, named after the bronze objects found in it, and the road ends at the Little Palace, which is on the right of the road from Herakleion to Knossos.

Knossos, The miniature wall-painting of the Tripartite Shrine

According to ancient legends told by Homer and later picked up by Strabo, it was Tlepolemus, son of Heracles, who founded on the island of Rhodes only 18 kilometers away from the western coast of Asia Minor, the important settlements of **Lindos**, **Ialysos** and **Kameiros**. Other myths refer to a "physical" origin of the Island: born from the love between Helios (the Sun god who indeed became its protecting divinity) and the nymph Rhodia. Certainly the island, inhabited since the neolithic age, was settled during the IInd millenium BC by populations coming from Crete, than by Achaei and finally by Dorians who arrived around 1100 BC.

Only in more recent times (in 409 BC according to the ancient authors) the city Rhodes, from which the Island takes its name, was founded through the "synoecism" (i.e. amalgamation) of the three pre-existing neighbouring villages into the new center. The Island which is the largest of the Dodecanese or Southern Sporades, thanks to its position in the midst of the most important sea-trading routes played an important role in the Mediterranean commerce: for centuries it was able to maintain its independence and become a real "Free-port" of Antiquity. Even during the fighting between the successors of Alexander the Great for the dividing of his empire, Rhodes

Rhodes, the Temple of the Pythian Apollo

was an important reference point for the various fleets. First allied with the Romans in the victorious battle of Myonnesos against king Antiochus III of Syria (190 BC), afterwards it antagonised Rome who in 166 BC created a new Free Port at Delos. The progressive crisis that followed was not enough to lessen the memories of its lost power. The diplomacy and wisdom of the Rhodians has left a trace in the history of naval law: the present rules are still inspired by those of the medieval Italian maritime Republics which in turn were based on the ancient "*Lex Rhodia*", the body of laws and regulations which had been elaborated in antiquity on the island.

The following centuries are marked by the presence of the Knights Hospitaller of St. John of Jerusalem (who settle here in 1309: from thereon they are spoken as the "Knights of Rhodes"), to whom succeeded the Turkish domination, and after that, from 1912 until the Second World War, the Italian domination that extended over the entire Dodecanese.

Many architectural traces testify to these past events in the Island's monuments, buildings and artistic heritage. In the township of Rhodes we can admire the **port** and in particular the **Walled City**, a masterpiece of XV-XVIth century architecture, which was built by the Knights over the ancient city which was almost completely obliterated.

The **Acropolis** was raised over two terraces: on the upper one, over a construction of large square blocks, are visible three Doric columns from the **Temple of Athena and Zeus Polieus** (i.e. protector of the city); on the lower terrace are the remains of vast monuments like the **Gymnasium** and the **Stadium** together with the **Odeion**.

South-west of the city there remains, in the necropolis said of Acandia, the so-called **Tomb of the Ptolomies**, a remarkable monument constituted of a square plinth into which was set a sort of tumulus that supported a small woods: a typical Hellenistic mausoleum, with a plan that will be repeated during the imperial Roman age.

At **Lindos**, on the eastern coast, the **Acropolis**, that rose on a high rocky spur overlooking the sea, was a remarkable sight and housed, on various levels linked by monumental stairways, the **Sanctuary of Athena Lindia**; the temple, built in the IVth century BC rose inside a square porticoed court which was entered from a Doric stoa and through monumental propylaia.

During the Roman age a small tetrastyle (i.e. 4 columned) temple was built in front of the stoa.

On the western coast, the ruins of Ialysos are visible on a height presently called Filerimos, and belong mostly to a **temple** dedicated to **Athena Polias**. The temple was built towards the end of the IIIrd century BC over the remains of an older one, maybe dedicated to Helios by Phoenician sailors of which remain a few large floor slabs; on the slopes of the Filerimos there is a **monumental fountain**; in this very suggestive place were later built in the subsequent centuries, a **paleochristian church**, an orthodox monastery, the church of Our Lady of Filerimos; close by are the ruins of a byzantine fortress.

At **Kameiros**, non far away from the Knights castle, can be found the remains of the last of the Island's large ancient centers. The city dates back at least to the VIIth century BC; after having contributed to the birth of Rhodes it was granted a new urban plan (IVth century BC) that was probably inspired by that of the Island's new capital city. Here however the constructions are distributed over an extensive terraced slope: on top, northwards, is a large stoa, and going down there is an important residential quarter and, southwards, a vast public piazza.

Besides being famous for its urban planning and architecture, Rhodes was celebrated, in the Hellenistic and Roman ages, for its important school of sculpture that rivalled with that of Athens and Pergamon. The gigantic statue of the Colossus said to stand 30 meters high, a masterpiece created by Chares of Lindos (who was a disciple of Lysippos) today lost, was celebrated in antiquity as one of the world's Seven Marvels.

Lindos, view of the Acropolis

The stoa of the Acropolis

THESSALONICA

The city is said to have been founded on the site of a previous settlement called Therma in 315 BC by the Macedonian general Cassander, who named it Thessalonica after his wife, who was also the sister of Alexander the Great. According to a different tradition, the founder was actually Alexander's father, Philip II. Thessalonica, famous for its position on the Thermaic Gulf, boasted **mighty walls** which can still be recognized in some stretches, even though they were rebuilt on many occasions, especially in Byzantine times.

The most important ancient monuments date back to the Roman period, however. The city became the capital of the Roman province of Macedonia in 146 BC The city already enjoyed the advantages of a being good port on the gulf, but it was the construction of the Via Egnatia in 130 BC that secured the city's good fortune. This was the long road built by proconsul Gn. Egnatius to link Dyrrhachium (now Durrës) to Thrace. It went straight through Thessalonica, cutting it in two (as suggested by stratigraphic tests made under the present-day Thessaloniki, which partly covers the ancient city).

From the north one looked over the pulsing centre of the **agora**, of which we are familiar only with the monument known as "**Las Incantadas**" (the name derives from an old legend of the Ghetto, quarter of the Jews originally from Spain: over 20,000 Sephardim expelled from the Iberian Peninsula in 1492).

These are four piers which probably decorated, along with others like them, a monumental passageway between the agora and a nearby basilica. Each of them bore sculpted figures in high relief, on either side: Nike and a Maenad; Aura and Dionysus; one of the Dioscuri and Ariadne; and Ganymedes seized by Jupiter and Leda and the swan. The theories of their date are somewhat uncertain, ranging between the 2nd and the 4th centuries AD.

The most famous ancient monument is, however, one built at the beginning of the 4th century AD by one of the Emperor-Tetrarchs, Galerius, who established his headquarters here. The complex covers a fairly wide area and consists of a palace, a hippodrome and a rotunda (probably a mausoleum, later transformed into the church of St. George), and it is joined to the Via Egnatia by a fairly broad street with porticos. At the junction of the two roads there was a **great four-fronted arch**, of which two of the four piers remain. The monument was in honour of Galerius himself. The piers feature sketchy but lively sculpted scenes of the wars conducted by the emperor in the East, in Armenia and Adiabene. The other piers, now lost, portrayed his other campaigns.

In 380 Theodosius the Great made Christianity the official religion in an edict promulgated in Thessalonica

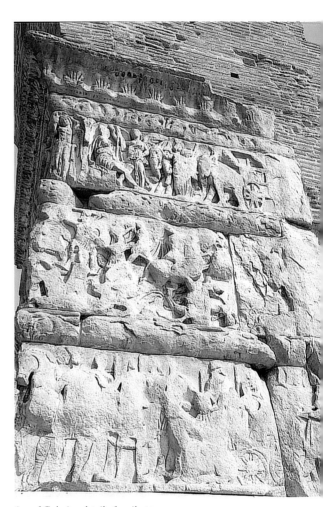

Arc of Galerius, detail of a pilaster

itself, which later became the second most important city in the Eastern Empire after Constantinople under Justinian. In the Byzantine period the city was adorned with beautiful churches often containing wonderful mosaics.

Detail of a mosaic with the portrait of Ariadne (Thessalonica, Archaeological Museum)

TIRYNS

Tiryns is located in the Peloponnese, in the east of Argolis, about 15 km from Mycenae.

Proitos, its founder and first king, is reputed to have entrusted the construction of its megalithic walls to the Cyclops, gigantic one-eyed herdsmen of massive strength of the likes of Polyphemos, who was made famous by Homer in the Odyssey. The fourth king, after Proitos, Perseus and Amphitryon was Heracles, the much-venerated hero (son of Zeus and Alcmene, to whom Amphitryon was married). It was here that he undertook his famous "twelve labours" at the behest of Eurystheus, king of Mycenae.

Whether or not they were built by the Cyclops, the **great walls**, of which long stretches are preserved, are truly amazing. They rise on a small hill at a distance of about 1,500 metres from the coast. The walls which can be seen today, built on top of previous structures, are in enormous roughly hewn blocks and are on average 6 metres wide and at certain points 10 metres tall. They contain galleries and casemates with lancet pseudo-vaults, obtained with progressive corbelling. Completed in around 1400 BC (Late Bronze Age), they contain a palace of Mycenaean type. In the late 13th century they were extended to the north, bringing the perimeter to about 700 metres and embracing an area (the "lower rock", which contained no buildings) the function of which was presumably to shelter the inhabitants of the surrounding areas in the event of enemy attack.

The **palace**, which is defended by a second ring of smaller, inner walls, also underwent different phases of construction. It attained its current, definitive form in around 1200 BC. On the east side, between the outer and the inner walls (which run parallel here) there was a checkpoint controlled by a gate, upon the threshold of which the holes of the doors are still preserved.

The large building develops along a central axis consisting of a **great courtyard** and the **king's megaron**. The megaron, as was habitual, consisted of three parts: a porch with two wooden columns (of which the stone bases remain); a *prodromos*, or anteroom, reached through a wall containing three doors; and a great hall with a central hearth (eschare) surrounded by four columns. There was a similar, smaller room immediately to the right of this (the **queen's megaron**) and other courtyards and rooms down the sides of the central axis.

Not long after the palace was finished, Tiryns was destroyed in the invasion of the Dorians, a people who arrived from the Balkans and contributed, here as elsewhere, to the collapse of the Mycenaean world. The city would never return to its previous splendour.

The village of Verghina, which lies on the plain of river Haliacmon (prefecture of Imathia to the south-west of Thessalonica), corresponds to the ancient Aigai, cradle of the royal dynasty of the kings of Macedonia, the Argeads. Founded in the 7th century BC by the semi-legendary progenitor Perdiccas I, it preserves a palace and a royal burial ground, with splendid tombs dug inside large burial mounds (over three hundred!), representing one of the most important archaeological discoveries of the 20th century.

The **palace** as we know it, the ruins of which lie in the area of Palatitsa, was probably built by Antigonos Gonatas (320-239 BC) over the site of a previous building. The numerous rooms are arranged around a large courtyard with porticoes which is reached from the outside through three successive anterooms; immediately to the left of this entrance is a round hall of which there have been various interpretations (sanctuary, throne room, banqueting hall); most probably it was a shrine consecrated to Heracles Patroos, protector of the sovereigns of Macedonia. The basic design of the palace of Verghina is echoed in that of Pella and in various Hellenistic royal residences.

The tombs inside what is known as the **Great Tumulus** are particularly noteworthy. The most important is attributed to Philip II (382-336 BC), the king who imposed Macedonian supremacy over the whole of Greece at the battle of Chaironeia against the Athenians in 338. His son, Alexander the Great, inherited a strong state organization, a powerful army and a policy which Alexander was to carry to its final conclusion: the war against the Persians. The tomb, which may have been built by the great heir himself, features a magnificently decorated architectural facade: solid piers at the two ends, engaged columns at either side of the doorway, lintel, Doric frieze and, above, a painted frieze (attributed to the painter Nikias) depicting Philip II and his sons engaged in hunting a lion. The interior consists of a burial chamber preceded by an anteroom. Objects of exceptional value have been found in the chamber: gold burial chests (one of which, resting inside a marble sarcophagus, contained the bones of the deceased wrapped in a pall of purple and gold), a wooden funerary bed decorated with ivory heads (two of which appear to represent Philip and Alexander), ceremonial weapons in iron and gold, and tableware in silver and bronze.

The anteroom also contained a gold box inside a marble sarcophagus, which also contained an impressive treasure (including a gold crown): this may have belonged to one of the king's concubines. Other noteworthy monumental tombs are: the one known as the **Prince's Tomb**, which may have belonged to Alexander IV, son of Alexander the Great, which contains a painted frieze depicting chariot races; another with a large fresco of the rape of Persephone; the **Tomb of Eurydice** (c. 340 BC) with a facade of four engaged Ionic columns, in front of which a marble throne was found; and other architectural and pictorial masterpieces.

Verghina, façade of a Macedonian tomb

The Rape of Persephone,
painting from the tomb of Philip II

Verghina,
small golden funerary chest

contents